Published in the United States by
Ancora Publishing
21 West 6th Avenue
Eugene, Oregon 97401
ancorapublishing.com

The Third Quest Student Reader
ISBN: 978-1-59909-093-1
Part of The Third Quest Student Materials
ISBN: 978-1-59909-090-0

Cover by Nick Siegrist
Book design and layout by Natalie Conaway

Marilyn Sprick and Ann Watanabe

We appreciate our story and student consultants,
who inspired us with their enthusiasm, engagement,
and creative thinking.

STORY CONSULTANTS
Anna Bell Herzig
Sione Kefu Halaliku
Hoʻohieokalā Luna-Beamer

STUDENT CONSULTANTS
Jasmine Graham
Cody Huffman
Arabella Kargel
Ronaldo Lopez

CHAPTERS

Level 1 Scientific Thinking

Level 2 Earth's History

Level 3 Age of Mammals

Level 4 Mesopotamia

Level 5 Ancient Egypt

Level 6 The Indus Valley and Ancient China

Level 7 Ancient Greece

Level 8 Ancient Rome

CHAPTER ONE

Upside Down

Narrative Fiction

Everything was upside down and inside out. What did the school board know about kids and neighborhoods? The neighborhoods had been divided, and kids were being sent to schools all over the city. No one knew anyone.

People were mad. Parents were mad. Teachers were mad. The kids were mad. Friends were split up.

The plan made no sense. The school board didn't understand. Social groups were gone. Everyone felt uncomfortable.

Mindy's "new" school was old and decrepit. Mindy walked to her first- and second-period block — English and History. The teacher was at the door. Mindy thought, **"She looks mean and cranky."**

Mindy made her way past the teacher and looked around. A few kids were talking, but it was spooky. The room was too quiet. •• Use four words or phrases to describe Mindy's new school. •• Describe Mindy's mood or how she feels.

Mindy took her seat. She was sitting near a skinny kid reading a book. Mindy thought, "That's odd. **Who still**

reads books?"

Gradually the room filled. The teacher's name was written on the screen at the front of the class — Ms. X. What kind of name was that? **The teacher clapped her hands.**

Mindy thought, "Really?" But the room got quiet. Usually everyone kept talking, but everyone just sat there. **No one was happy.**

Ms. X said, "I need your attention." Then she waited until everyone was listening. **Ms. X said, "I am old, mean, and cranky. I can see that you are mad, but you are stuck with me."**

Mindy was thinking, "This is bad. This is so bad. No one should have to go to this old school!"

The teacher continued, "Being sent to this school is unfair, but that isn't relevant. You are going to learn about what existed before you. You will study history and learn!" •• What does Ms. X think is relevant or important? •• Why are the kids upset? •• Based on what you know, describe Ms. X.

The girl in the seat next to Mindy rolled her eyes. **She muttered, "The past! I wish we could just skip this class. The past is the past. No one wants to study the past."**

Ms. X glared at the girl. Then she pointed at her and said, "You should listen." Next, Ms. X said without expression, "This class has been selected to send a group into the past. A Quest has not been held for a hundred years. The last Quest team did not return." There was a moment of silence as the kids thought about what the teacher had said.

A kid began to mutter, "No one is going to want to go."

But the lanky kid near Mindy sat up and said, "That

means that . . ." Then the kid started talking really fast. Words seemed to fall out of his mouth. "Quest? The first group that went on a time quest visited the dinosaurs, went on a mammoth hunt, built a pyramid, and . . ." Suddenly, the kid seemed to notice that everyone was staring at him, so he stopped. •• Describe the kid. •• Does the Quest sound interesting? Why or why not?

Ms. X looked at the kid. "Mr. Tuppins, is it? A team from this class will go deep, deep into the past."

Ms. X continued, "Knowledge will be important. The selected travelers will need to work as a group or there will be another unfortunate outcome."

Mindy listened to the teacher's ominous words and thought, "Unfortunate outcomes, group work — group work never works!" •• What makes the teacher's words ominous?

Ms. X said, "One team will go into the past. In fact, it will be a team of six. I wish I was going, but I can't."

Mindy looked around at the others and thought. "This can't be real." Zack and Lambert were the only other kids from Hill Academy. Mindy thought, "Zack is okay, but there is no way I'm going to time travel with Lambert or strangers." **Mindy said, "I pass. I don't want to go into the past. Dad will . . ."**

Before Mindy could finish, Ms. X was reading names — "J.T. Tuppins, Shack Jones, Ling Roberts, Zack Jefferson, Anna Gomez, Mindy Herzig." •• Was Mindy picked to go on the Quest? •• Do you think Mindy will go? Why or why not?

Ms. X said, "You are lucky. Tuppins will go with you. You will need him." Tuppins seemed glad to go. He was grinning from ear to ear. The past was his thing.

Mindy said, "Have fun." •• Does Mindy think she is going?

Ms. X said, "You are going to the past. You will need to think. You will need to work as a team. Use your heads, or no good will come of this." •• What do you think Ms. X means? •• Would you want to go on the Quest? Why or why not?

CHAPTER TWO

A Privilege?

Narrative Fiction

Everything went totally quiet. The air was strangely warm and damp. Mindy found herself staring at the odd kid from class.

Tuppins was looking at something. It was an armored frog-like creature.

Mindy rubbed her eyes and shook her head. The frog-like creature was still there. **It didn't look happy.** Mindy covered her eyes and shook her head again. **She looked up. There was still no class and no mean teacher. Just Tuppins — that kid from class — and he was grinning.** •• Why does Mindy keep rubbing her eyes? •• How do you know that Mindy and Tuppins have begun the Quest?

Mindy thought, **"This must be a dream. It can't be real. Can it?" But it was. There were no people — just Tuppins and her.** Then Mindy remembered that Ms. X had said, "Use your heads." Finally, she heard herself talking. **"So, Tuppins, where are we?"**

Still grinning, Tuppins said, "Judging from the presence of the *Beelzebufo ampinga* (bee-el-zi-BOOF-oh am-PING-uh),

I believe we must be somewhere in Madagascar 65 to 70 million years ago."

Mindy looked at Tuppins and said, "You can't be happy, can you? This isn't fun, and that thing you are looking at isn't happy."

Tuppins grinned. "You are probably quite right. Also known as the devil frog, *Beelzebufo ampinga* was thought to be quite mean. He was the descendant of frogs that began appearing 180 million years ago. *Beelzebufo ampinga* was thought to have weighed about ten pounds and . . ."

Mindy thought, "How odd," but she just said, "So the frog is ancient, but how do we get back?"

Tuppins said, "I don't think you understand. We can't just go back." •• How does Tuppins know they were 65 to 70 million years in the past? •• Why does Mindy think that it is odd for Tuppins to talk on and on about the frog?

Mindy said, "You don't understand. We need to go back."
Tuppins said, "To go back, we will have things to do."

Mindy said, "You are right. I don't get it. What are we supposed to do?"

Tuppins said, "That isn't clear to me. The Quest is a privilege. We were selected to represent our generation." •• Why does Tuppins think the Quest is a privilege?

Mindy was stunned. According to Tuppins, they were stuck somewhere 65 million years ago on some Quest. Tuppins seemed to think it was fun and had no idea how to get back.

Mindy began thinking, "No people, no teachers, no kids, no parents — just Tuppins? What do I know about 65 million years ago? Dinosaurs — big meat-eating dinosaurs! And they all went extinct around 65 million years ago."

Mindy said, "No dinos, no Tuppins, NO MINDY! This is bad!"

Tuppins finished Mindy's thinking. He said, "Scientists agree that a huge asteroid hit the Earth around this time. That event was a major factor in ending the rule of the dinosaurs."

Mindy shook her head thinking about the ominous event. Asteroid strikes Earth! Poof! •• Why did Mindy say, "This is bad"? •• What ominous event threatens Mindy and Tuppins? •• What does Tuppins think about their situation?

Tuppins said, "After the asteroid hit, earthquakes, tsunamis, and volcanic eruptions followed. Rampant fires and acid rain would have immediately killed living things. Then, for 32,000 years, species around the world died out."

Suddenly, the ground began to tremble. Mindy began to panic. She said, "Tuppins, look at me! This is bad. We have to do something." It was clear to her. They could be killed with the dinos.

Tuppins looked at Mindy. "The *Beelzebufo*'s relatives live in South America."

Mindy said, "Look at me, Tuppins. We need a plan for going back. The frog isn't relevant. The Quest isn't relevant. Who cares about winning a big prize?"

Tuppins looked startled and said, "There is no prize. •• Is the frog relevant or important to Mindy? Why or why not?

Tuppins said, "Reporters said that people filled the streets. They clapped for the team of 2100. In 2200, the team

didn't come back. Search teams were sent across time, but the team was never found."

Mindy said, "So, if we don't finish . . ." •• What is Mindy thinking? •• Describe Mindy. •• Would you rather be stranded with Tuppins or Mindy? Why?

Afterword

Mindy and Tuppins had traveled millions of years into the past. If there had been a choice, Mindy would have stayed in the year 2300. But Tuppins, who rarely thought about consequences, would have chosen the Quest — simply because it was a quest. •• Describe a quest.

Tuppins determined that he and Mindy had traveled across time to Madagascar, 65–70 million years ago. •• What was his evidence?

1. The landscape
2. The frog-like creature
3. The trembling of the Earth

CHAPTER THREE

Giant "Devil Frog" Discovered

Informational

Illustration by Lucille Betti-Nash / Used with permission

Congratulations. To get to this point in the Quest, your team has been successful. To move forward, you have a new challenge.

You will need to pass a quiz. The topic is Earth's history. Listen and read carefully. There is much to learn. •• Why do you need to listen and read carefully?

• • •

Fossils reveal the Earth's history. •• What do fossils reveal or tell?

In 1993, a research team from New York discovered the fossils of a giant frog that lived 65 to 70 million years ago. The bones were found in Madagascar, a large island off the east coast of Africa.

Look at the map. Find Africa. Point to the island off the coast of Africa. •• What is the name of this island? •• What did the research team from New York discover in Madagascar in 1993?

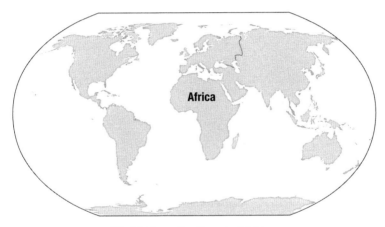

World Map, Continent of Africa

Hunting and Studying Fossils

The research team traveled back and forth from the United States to Madagascar. In 2008, fifteen years after their first trip, the researchers reported their findings to the world. **They had dug up fossil bits from a monster frog that lived 65 to 70 million years ago!**

For years the researchers gathered and studied fossil pieces. Although many pieces of the gigantic frog's skeleton were missing, scientists were able to determine what the frog may have looked like.

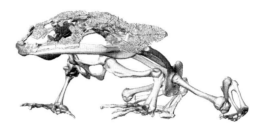

CT scan by Joe Groenke / © 2014 Evans et al. Used with permission

Fossils suggested the frog was a giant. It was thought to be 16 inches long and weigh about 10 pounds.

From 75 fossil bits, the researchers built a model. Next, an artist created an illustration of the ancient frog.

•• Let's explain how fossils can reveal the appearance of an animal that lived millions of years ago. First, the scientists found fossil pieces. Then what did they do?

Fossils revealed that the frog had an armored shield on its head, a wide mouth, and powerful jaws. This suggested that the frog ate lizards, snakes, small mammals, and perhaps even baby dinosaurs. •• **Did the researchers think the monster frog was . . .**

1. a plant eater?
2. a meat eater?
3. a plant and meat eater?

•• What evidence or facts support your answer?

Beelzebufo Ampinga

The frog was given the scientific name *Beelzebufo* (bee-el-zi-BOOF-oh) *ampinga*. Its name comes from Greek and Latin words that mean "devil," "toad," and "shield." **This monster frog is often referred to as the devil frog.** •• Why did scientists choose a name that means devil frog?

Knowledge Evolves

Informational

In 1993, a research team from the United States found fossil bits from a monster frog that lived 65 to 70 million years ago. The research team did not stop looking for more fossils. They wanted to learn more about the devil frog and other animals from the past. They traveled back to Madagascar, digging for more fossils. In 2014, the research team reported that they had learned more about the devil frog.

The scientists learned that the devil frog was smaller than originally thought. Instead of 16 inches wide, *Beelzebufo* may have been only about 7.5 inches wide. •• After finding more fossils, what did the research team report in 2014?

Despite its smaller size, the devil frog was still found to be an ominous creature.

- It had massive spikes sticking out of its huge skull.
- Its head was almost all mouth.
- Its mouth was filled with plate-like teeth.
- It was heavily armored with plates embedded in the skin of its back and head.

The passage says the frog had massive spikes sticking out of its skull. •• What do you think "massive spikes" means? •• Explain why scientists thought the devil frog was an ominous creature. •• Look at the illustration on page 9 again. If the artist changed the picture, what would she need to add?

Science Evolves

Researchers study and link facts together. They learn from the past.

Over time, knowledge grows. Sometimes new facts change our conclusions. Sometimes facts verify what we know.

Between 2008 and 2014, scientists verified that:

- **The devil frog was a meat eater.**
- **The devil frog looked mean.**
- **The devil frog was bigger than most modern frogs.**

Facts are important. They lead to deep thinking and questions. •• What did the researchers verify or prove about the frog?

When things change over time, they evolve. New facts change knowledge. •• What does knowledge do over time?

Questions from Research

Ancient devil frog fossils may seem unimportant. However, the knowledge learned is important. **The researchers learned facts about Earth's history.**

Fact 1. Fossils of the devil frog were found on Madagascar, an island off the coast of Africa.

Fact 2. The devil frog lived 65 to 70 million years ago.

Fact 3. A modern-day South American frog is the descendant of the devil frog.

The facts raise important questions about Earth's history.

Look at the map.

1. Find Africa.

2. **Find Madagascar.**

3. **Find South America.**

4. Put your finger on Madagascar. •• How do you think the frog got to South America?

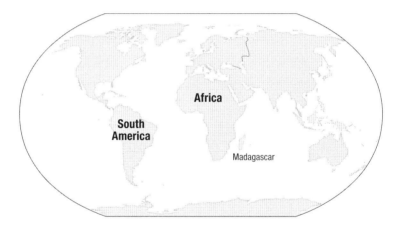

•• What questions do you have about the *Beelzebufo ampinga*? Start with: I wonder . . .

CHAPTER FIVE

Unlocking Earth's Mysteries

Informational

You learned that scientific knowledge about the devil frog evolved. •• How did knowledge of the devil frog evolve or change over time?

Your team has worked together. You have persevered. You have learned a lot. You will need to pass a quiz. The topic is unlocking the history of the Earth.

• • •

To unlock the past, scientists:

1. Observe
2. Ask questions
3. **Form hypotheses** or educated guesses
4. Test their hypotheses
5. Draw conclusions

The steps repeat. The process is called the scientific method. **As facts are learned, scientists understand more about Earth's history.**

Steps in the Scientific Method

This chart shows the scientific method. Touch each step as we read. There are five steps.

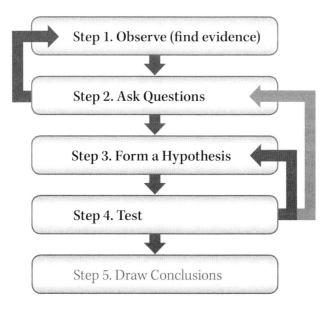

•• What do you think the arrows show?

The Scientific Method at Work

Step 1. Observe. In 1993, a team of scientists led by David Krause discovered the fossils of an ancient frog in Madagascar. **The fossils were 65 to 70 million years old.** Scientists studied the devil frog and determined it was the relative of a modern-day South American frog. •• What was the first step in the scientific method?

Step 2. Ask questions. Scientists asked, "What was a South American frog doing in Madagascar 65 to 70 million years ago? **How did the devil frog travel from Madagascar to South**

America?" •• What questions did the scientists ask?

Step 3. Form a hypothesis. Some people suggested that the devil frog swam across the ocean from Madagascar to South America. •• What hypothesis was suggested by some people?

Step 4. Test. Scientists know that frogs and toads cannot swim across oceans. **The devil frog did not swim across seas. This hypothesis did not stand up to the facts.** •• How do we know the devil frog didn't swim to South America?

Step 3. Form a different hypothesis. Perhaps the *Beelzebufo*'s relatives crossed from Madagascar to South America by a land connection 65 to 70 million years ago.

Step 4. Test. Most scientists agree that Madagascar was not connected to land 65 to 70 million years ago. In fact, scientists think Madagascar has been an island for 88 million years. **This hypothesis has not stood up.** •• Why do scientists think the frog did not travel by land from Madagascar to South America 65 to 70 million years ago?

Step 3. Form a different hypothesis. Scientists think the devil frog has lived on Earth longer than we think. Perhaps the devil frog lived in Madagascar more than 88 million years ago — before Madagascar was an island. If so, the ancient devil frogs could have made their way to South America by land.

Step 4. Test. Scientists need to find fossils of the *Beelzebufo* that are more than 88 million years old.

Step 5. Draw conclusions. Scientists have not found fossils of the *Beelzebufo*'s relatives that are 88 million years old. Scientists cannot prove how *Beelzebufo*'s relatives got from

Madagascar to South America. **They need more evidence.**
•• What would prove that the devil frog's relatives traveled to South America before Madagascar became an island?

Mysteries

Sometimes, we find the answers to mysteries from the past. Over time, scientists make more observations. **More questions are asked. More hypotheses are tested.** Perseverance pays off and mysteries are solved. But other mysteries stay locked in Earth's 4.6-billion-year history. •• What do scientists do to solve the mysteries of the past? •• Name the steps in the scientific method.

CHAPTER SIX

Perseverance

Informational

Building Background Knowledge

Look at Map 1. It is a map of the world today. Can you find the seven continents?

1. **Find North America.**

2. **Find South America.**

3. Point to Africa, Asia, Australia, and Antarctica.

4. Now find Europe.

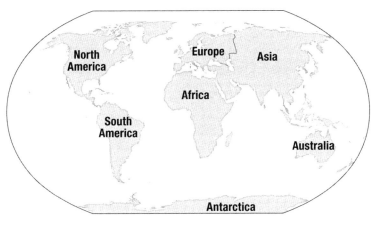

Map 1, Earth today

Revealing Earth's Ancient History

In the 1900s (about a hundred years ago), a German scientist named Alfred Wegener observed that similar animal fossils were found in Africa and South America. **Wegener asked, "Could animals have traveled from one continent to the other?" His answer: The animals could have traveled across the continents if there had been just one big continent.**

Wegener thought the continents fit together like a big puzzle. **Think of the continents as a big puzzle.** Look at Map 1 again. •• Does it look like Africa and South America fit together?

In 1915, Wegener wrote a book about his hypothesis. **In his book, Wegener said that millions of years ago there had been one big continent on Earth. He said the continents must have been one landmass, not seven.**

Wegener named this supercontinent Pangea (Greek for "all Earth"). Wegener thought that Pangea slowly separated into seven continents. He thought the Earth's rotation caused the continents to drift. •• What was Wegener's hypothesis?

Wegener was laughed at. **He could not test his hypothesis,** but Wegener never gave up believing that there had been one supercontinent. Today we know Wegener's theory was partially right, just ahead of its time. •• How did Wegener demonstrate perseverance?

Earth Facts

This is a fact about Earth. The continents do drift. The continents sit on massive slabs of rock. The huge slabs of rock, or plates, lie on the Earth's surface. The plates are continually moving, causing earthquakes, volcanoes, and a gradual shifting of the continents. The movement of the plates is called plate tectonics.

Look at Map 2. Earth had one vast landmass 250 million years ago. •• What do you notice about South America and Africa?

Map 2, Pangea (Earth 250 million years ago)

Fossils tell us that animals traveled across Pangea. This explains why dinosaur fossils are found in Antarctica. It also may help explain why the *Beelzebufo* had descendants who live in South America today.

First, Pangea split into two landmasses. **After millions of years, the two big landmasses drifted into the seven continents.**

Look back at Map 1 (Earth today). Today, North America and Europe are moving away from each other by about an inch each year.

Look back at Map 2. The continents are not still. They keep drifting. There have been four supercontinents in

Earth's history. In fact, scientists think there will be another supercontinent in 100 million years! •• Stop and think. If you were alive 100 million years from now, how many continents would there be?

Afterword

Plate tectonics was not widely accepted as fact until the 1960s, long after Wegener's death. He is now famous for his observations, questions, and hypothesis. **Wegener was a great thinker.** •• Why do people still talk about Wegener 100 years later?

Quiz

Here's your quiz. This time, you can look back in the text for help. Beware. Later you will need to answer these questions without help.

1. **What are the seven continents?**
2. Name the five steps in the scientific method.

CHAPTER SEVEN

The Rules

Narrative Fiction

Mindy was beginning to panic, but the devil frog was distracting her. The frog seemed to be sitting on something.

Mindy said, "Tuppins, look! That frog is sitting on some-thing. It's a pink folder." •• What do you think is in the folder?

Tuppins peered under the frog and said, "In all probability, *Beelzebufo* is sitting and waiting for something to eat. Scientists think that the frog would sit and wait, and then attack its prey."

Mindy said, "Tuppins, we need to see what's in the folder."

Tuppins said, "The *Beelzebufo* will snap at meat that comes near. If you offer the frog your hand, he will have it for dinner."

Mindy looked at Tuppins. "Focus. We need that folder!" Mindy was getting sick to her stomach. •• Why is Mindy feeling sick?

But she mumbled, "Think, Mindy, think! Don't panic. That would not be good."

Mindy asked, "If I sneak in back of the frog, do you think I could grab the folder?"

Tuppins said, "Scientists have no way to determine what the *Beelzebufo*'s eyesight might have been like. However, if it's like a modern-day frog, the *Beelzebufo* can see in back of itself." •• Will the information that Tuppins shared about the frog help Mindy? How? •• Is the information relevant?

Tuppins went on. "Meat in any form would be a great snack. Your hand or foot would appeal to the frog."

Mindy grabbed a big leaf and offered it to the frog. The frog just sat there looking mean. •• Why do you think the leaf did not distract the frog?

Mindy took a deep breath and said, "Okay, I get it. Short of offering the frog my hand, what can we give him?"

Tuppins said, "The *Beelzebufo* has a big mouth and powerful jaws, so scientists think it would have eaten lizards and other small animals."

Mindy looked up and jumped. Shack and Ling were standing near her. Shack was looking at the frog, too. He started to say something, but he just closed his mouth.

Ling looked grim. Tuppins just shrugged. Mindy was relieved but didn't know what to say. •• Why do you think Mindy is relieved?

Finally, Shack broke the silence. Shack said, "So this is the Quest thing."

Mindy nodded. "We think we are stuck somewhere millions of years ago."

Shack asked, "So what's with the mean frog?"

Mindy said, "He has a folder. It has to be for us. We need

that folder." Mindy started to point at the *Beelzebufo*, but it was gone. **Mindy grabbed the folder and began reading.**

To: The Travelers
From: Quest Central
Date: **The year 2300**
Subject: Quest 2300

You have entered Quest 2300. Travelers who return from the Quest will be heroes and justly rewarded.

Teams who do not finish the Quest will vanish.

You have been picked! As a traveler, you will cross millions of years of history.

If your team follows the rules, the odds will be in your favor.

The Quest Rules are:

1. Follow directions.
2. **Stick together.**
3. Do your part.
4. Be respectful.
5. Stay cool and calm.

•• What does the team need to do to get back?

Shack muttered something. He looked grim. Then he said, "Who follows rules?"

Mindy said, "If you don't, we will vanish. Tuppins thinks we've been transported to 65 to 70 million years ago. No

people — just us, the frog, and perhaps some dinosaurs."

Shack stared at his three classmates and started thinking about extinction.

Shack said, "If it's 65 million years ago, we are good, but if it's 66 million years ago . . ." Then Shack looked at Ling. **She was in a panic and looked as if she was going to scream.**

Shack said, "Hey, it says you got to be cool and calm. Take a deep breath." •• Shack changed his tune very quickly. Why do you think he decided it was important to follow the rules?

Ling nodded.

Mindy thought, "Shack talks big, but he will be okay. **He won't get rattled. That's important.**" Then she thought, "**I really wish we were back at school with the mean old teacher.**"

Suddenly two figures came walking down the sandy beach.

They were Zack and Anna. Zack acted as if nothing had happened. He seemed aloof. Anna looked calm but worried. •• Describe how Zack is behaving.

The kids had been transported back in time 65 to 70 million years. •• Which students almost panicked? Which students were calm?

CHAPTER EIGHT

Survival

Narrative Fiction

Previously in the Third Quest

The Important When: 65 to 70 million years ago
The Important Where: Madagascar

Madagascar

T he team was complete. •• What do you think the team needs to do to survive?

• • •

Mindy looked at Tuppins and thought, **"Tuppins is a walking Internet. He is different but smart."** •• Will Tuppins be an asset? Why?

Mindy surveyed the rest of the group. **Zack would be an asset. He had gone to school with her.** He was captain of the Hill Academy football team. But what about the others? **She had been class president at Hill.** She wondered, "Is that why I was chosen?"

Mindy could hear herself telling the others about the memo. Everyone but Shack read the rules again.

1. Follow directions.
2. **Stick together.**
3. **Do your part.**
4. **Be respectful.**
5. Stay cool and calm.

•• Name the five rules. •• Which student didn't read the rules again? •• Why do you think that might be a problem?

Then Anna said, "I had this in my pocket." It was another memo.

> **To:** The Travelers
> **From:** Quest Central
> **Date:** **The year 2300**
> **Subject: Task 1, Quest 2300**
>
> Task 1. Watch for your basic survival needs. **Find fresh air, food, clean water, and shelter.**
>
> Remember the rules. The rules are not to be broken.

•• What does the team need to find? •• Is this an ominous sign, or is it exciting? Why?

Anna said, "It sounds like we are on our own. **Where are we?"**

Tuppins grinned and began talking. "So, the presence of the *Beelzebufo ampinga* has led us to conclude that we are in Madagascar right around 65 to 70 million years ago."

Anna said, "That's about the time the dinosaurs went extinct."

Tuppins said, "That would be correct."

Ling said, "I think this could be bad for us."

Tuppins said, "Some animals lived. The *Beelzebufo* survived. Insects, frogs, snakes, lizards, most birds, and some small mammals survived. Scientists estimate that 71%–81% of all species died out, including the dinosaurs."

Ling said, "Tuppins, that isn't good. If we are in the middle of the K-T extinction, animals over 50 pounds died."

Mindy thought, "I weigh 102 pounds." She watched as the others thought about the impending loss of life.

The sky had gotten dark. A toxic smell began to permeate the air. •• What is ominous?

Shack began walking. Mindy and the others followed Shack. Finally, Mindy asked, "Do you know where you are going?"

Shack said calmly, "No, I don't know. **That memo said to find food, water, shelter, and air. So that's what we are doing. We have to try.** Standing around didn't seem to be getting us anywhere."

Mindy nodded. She had thought Shack might be a problem, but he wasn't going to stand around and do nothing. **Shack was going to be an asset.** •• Why does Mindy think that?

CHAPTER NINE

The Team of Six

Narrative Fiction

Previously in the Third Quest
The Important When: Millions of years ago
The Important Where: Madagascar

The sky was dark. A toxic smell permeated the air. **A memo said the team needed to find fresh air, clean water, food, and shelter.** Shack didn't know where to go, but he led the way.

• • •

Dust began to fill the air. Tuppins said, "Sixty-six million years ago, an asteroid crashed to Earth and made a huge 112-mile crater off the coast of Mexico. Chunks from the meteorite sent poisonous gases into the air."

Anna asked, "Is that what's happening?" An acrid smell was filling the air. •• What do you think acrid means? What in the text makes you think that?

Tuppins said, "I can't be sure, but it would appear we have arrived during the K-T extinction."

Shack said, "Then we do need to find fresh air, food, clean water, and shelter."

Ling said, "I think I saw a cave earlier. Shack, did you see it? It was near where we were transported."

Before anyone could respond, Shack took off running. Mindy, Ling, Tuppins, Anna, and Zack fell in behind him. Finally Shack slowed down and waited for Ling to point out the cave. •• How did Ling and Shack help the team?

The team entered. It was dark. But the air was fresh. Shack walked into the darkness and disappeared. Not long after, he hollered to them, "There's a stream!"

The kids stumbled after Shack. They linked hands and walked together until they got to Shack. They cupped their hands and drank the fresh water. •• How did Shack help the group?

They followed the stream until they stumbled into a room dimly lit by the hazy daylight. Mindy thought, "This is great." But then she looked at Zack. He was acting kind of funny. He still seemed aloof. He seemed flat. His lack of expression reminded Mindy of her android.

Mindy wished she had her droid. A droid would have gotten them food. Then this strange but fleeting thought came to Mindy. She started to think, "Could Zack be a . . . ?" •• What do you think Mindy is thinking?

Before she could finish her thought, Anna emerged from a tunnel. She was grinning. She had six big eggs. They were so big she struggled not to drop them. Anna said, "There was a nest — dino eggs!" •• How did Anna help the group?

Everyone was hungry. Mindy wondered what they were

going to do with raw dino eggs. At home, the droids brought them whatever they wanted, ready to eat.

Ling said, "I can cook, but I need heat and a pan or something."

Shack said, "We could just eat the eggs. They don't need to be cooked." Anna handed Shack an uncooked egg. Shack looked at the big egg and said, "I'm good with cooked."

Mindy looked for Zack. He was off to the side of the cave. He had lit a fire under a thin slab of rock! •• How did Zack light the fire?

Ling cooked one egg at a time. Everyone was quiet as they ate. Mindy was impressed with the group. •• Why is Mindy impressed with the group?

But the rumbling of the Earth continued, and there seemed to be fires in the distance.

Shack said, "That memo said, 'Get yourself shelter, air, water, and food.' We got the shelter. We got the air. We got fresh water, and we got food."

Shack had barely ticked off their accomplishments when he noticed it was so cold that he could see his breath. The air had been hot, then suddenly cold. •• What do you think is happening? Why do you think that?

Afterword

•• Is Tuppins odd? What makes you think that?

•• Is Shack an asset? Why or why not?

Anna is bold. •• What in the text supports that conclusion?

1. She screamed.

2. She made fire.
3. She went exploring and found food.

•• What word best describes Ling? Why?

1. Spoiled
2. **Helpful**
3. **Stuck up**

Zack is aloof. •• What in the text supports that conclusion?

1. He is captain of the football team.
2. He has no expression and seems flat.
3. He is a droid.

CHAPTER TEN

The Scientific Method

Informational

Scientists use the scientific method to learn more about Earth. There are five basic steps.

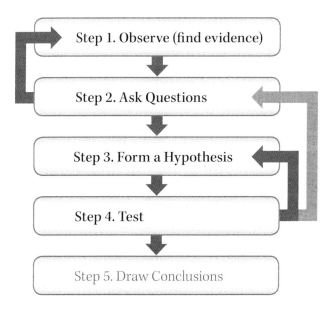

Step 1. Observe (find evidence)

Step 2. Ask Questions

Step 3. Form a Hypothesis

Step 4. Test

Step 5. Draw Conclusions

Look at Step 4. •• Trace the arrows. If the test fails to prove a hypothesis, what do scientists do?

Yes, the steps are recursive. **They repeat.** Scientists use the steps in the scientific method to solve mysteries. **One of Earth's biggest mysteries is what killed the dinosaurs?**

Steps in the Scientific Method

Step 1. Observe. Layers of rock lie under the Earth's surface. **From fossil evidence, scientists have observed that the dinosaurs lived on Earth for about 170 million years.**

A wide variety of dinosaurs traveled across all seven continents. **Some were plant eaters, and others were meat eaters.** There were gentle, plodding giants and bloodthirsty hunters.

Then about 66 million years ago, the dinosaurs started to disappear. But it wasn't just dinosaurs that died out. From fossil evidence, scientists know that about 75% of all plant and animal species went extinct along with the dinosaurs. **Plants and animals that lived on land went extinct, as did plants and animals in the sea.** •• When the dinosaurs went extinct, what else died out?

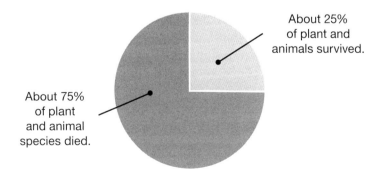

About 25% of plant and animals survived.

About 75% of plant and animal species died.

Step 2. Ask questions. For years, people asked questions. **Why did dinosaurs go extinct?** Why did they vanish after ruling the Earth for 170 million years? What caused their demise? •• What does the word "demise" mean?

Step 3. Form hypotheses. For years, scientists and other people formed many hypotheses about why dinosaurs went extinct.

Step 4. Test the hypotheses. Next, scientists had to prove which hypothesis was correct. Scientists looked for evidence to verify each hypothesis.

Step 5. Draw conclusions. Finally, scientists hoped to draw conclusions. Scientists need a mountain of evidence to prove a hypothesis. •• What do scientists need to prove a hypothesis?

Example: Too Big

In Steps 1 to 3, scientists observe, ask questions, and form a hypothesis. People observed that the dinosaurs had become huge. The Argentinosaurus was massive. Some were as tall as a six-story building. **Some were as long as three school buses. A hypothesis was formed.** The dinosaurs went extinct because they got too big to support their bodies. •• **What was the hypothesis?**

Tests. Facts ruled out this hypothesis. Fossils showed that dinosaurs of all sizes went extinct. This hypothesis did not explain why small dinosaurs went extinct. **It didn't answer why other plants and animals went extinct.** •• What was wrong with the hypothesis?

Conclusion: Scientists concluded that the dinosaurs did not go extinct because they got too big.

More Hypotheses

Scientists have formed other hypotheses about why the dinosaurs went extinct. Some of the hypotheses are:

- **Dinosaurs got sick.** Insects carried diseases that killed off the dinosaurs.
- **Dinosaurs were killed when a massive asteroid crashed into the earth.**
- Dinosaurs died out due to volcanic activity.
- **Dinosaur eggs were eaten by other animals.**
- Dinosaurs couldn't compete with mammals for food and died of starvation.

What is your hypothesis? •• What do you think killed off the dinosaurs?

Finding answers to scientific questions is hard work. To separate fact from opinion, scientists require a mountain of evidence. •• What does "a mountain of evidence" mean? •• Why do scientists need perseverance?

CHAPTER ELEVEN

A Mountain of Evidence

Informational

Layers of Rock

When scientists have questions about Earth's past, they look in the rocks. They dig deeper. The deeper they dig, the older the rocks. Each layer of rock reveals Earth's past. Look at the picture. Find the layer of rock where dinosaur fossils are found.

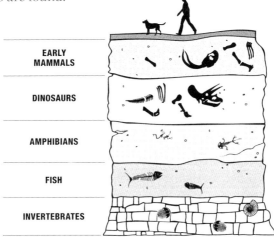

EARLY MAMMALS

DINOSAURS

AMPHIBIANS

FISH

INVERTEBRATES

Dinosaur fossils are found in rocks for about 170 million years of Earth's history. Then suddenly, there are no dinosaur

fossils. The dinosaurs were here and then they were gone. •• How long did the dinosaurs roam Earth?

The disappearance of the dinosaurs has been a great mystery. **It wasn't just the dinosaurs that vanished.** Most of the world's plant and animal species also went extinct. **People ask, "What killed the dinosaurs?** What killed 75% of all animal and plant species? **What happened 66 million years ago?"**

A Hypothesis Formed

In 1980 a scientist named Walter Alvarez found a metal called iridium. The iridium was found in a layer of Earth that was 66 million years old. Iridium is rare on Earth, but is found in space rocks and asteroids. **Together Walter and his father Luis hypothesized that the metal was evidence of a massive asteroid crashing into Earth. They formed a hypothesis. The dinosaurs went extinct when a massive asteroid crashed into Earth.** •• What was the hypothesis?

The scientists thought an asteroid crash could have triggered a mass extinction around the world. People laughed at the scientists. **They scoffed at the hypothesis. More evidence was needed.** •• What do you think "scoffed" means?

Scientists began looking for iridium in rock layers from Earth's past. **They found the metal in rocks around the world.** They found iridium from the time the dinosaurs disappeared. **Skeptics asked, "If there was an asteroid, where did it crash? Where's the crater?" More evidence was needed.** •• Why was more evidence needed?

The Evidence

In a mystery, a smoking gun is solid evidence in a case. The Alvarez team needed a smoking gun — proof that a huge asteroid had crashed into Earth. A crater would be the smoking gun. •• What proof was needed?

In the 1990s, scientists learned of a crater. The crater was found off the coast of Mexico. It was first discovered by an oil company. The massive crater is 112 miles wide. **The crater is as big as Mt. Everest. The crater supported the asteroid hypothesis.** •• What verified the hypothesis?

Look at the picture.

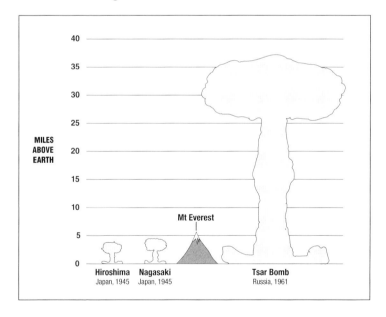

Find Mount Everest. Mt. Everest is the world's biggest mountain. Find the Russian nuclear bomb. In 1961, the Russians tested a bomb. The blast created a mushroom cloud that was 7 times higher than Mt. Everest.

The asteroid blast was 200 million times bigger than the Russian bomb! **The crash of the asteroid was massive.** The size of the blast is hard to imagine, but the results were catastrophic around the world. •• What did the blast create?

After the Blast

Scientists have used a computer model to verify what happened. The blast caused wildfires around the world. **The impact was massive.** The crash triggered volcanic eruptions, earthquakes, and tsunamis. **What happened after the asteroid struck Earth?** •• Close your eyes and try to imagine what was happening on Earth immediately after the asteroid struck.

For two years, the Earth was dark. The sky was filled with dust and ash. It got very, very cold. With no sun, plants and animals could not live. After the asteroid crashed into Earth, animals and plants went extinct across 32,000 years. •• How long did the extinction take?

Conclusions

Scientists have found evidence that huge volcanic eruptions started in India 150,000 years before the asteroid crash. **This volcanic activity increased after the asteroid hit Earth.**

From a mountain of evidence, scientists conclude that the asteroid strike and volcanic activity led to the demise of the dinosaurs. **As scientists keep learning more, our understanding of Earth's history keeps evolving.** •• What have scientists concluded? •• Do you think this conclusion may change? If so, why and how?

CHAPTER TWELVE

Morning Briefing

Narrative Fiction

The teacher from the decrepit school began each day the same way. **As was her habit, she was up at 6:00 a.m.** Her breakfast was served by a robot. **If anyone was observing, Ms. X seemed to be an ordinary person.**

After eating, Ms. X walked into her garden to feed her pet. It was still dark. Ms. X turned on the patio light. *Beelzebufo* was hidden somewhere in the plants. She left the frog a dish of meat. *Beelzebufo* liked to eat from Ms. X's hand, but she had work to do. **Ms. X walked to her den.** •• Do you think Ms. X is an ordinary person? Why or why not?

Ms. X said out loud, "What is happening this morning?" **The computer started up.** A large screen revealed more than a hundred emails. Ms. X said, "Quest Central," and her daily briefing opened. **Ms. X listened to the report.**

The Quest Times
Morning Briefing

Wednesday, September 12, 2300 | By Jamal West

Good morning. Here's what you need to know.

The Quest 2300 team sticks together

The Quest team is sticking together. As predicted, the team members are doing their parts. They are using their assets for the common good. •• How are the team members using their assets for the common good? Give examples.

Links:

> Hill Academy: Mindy and Zack
> **Public School 102: Tuppins and Ling**
> **Public School 201: Anna and Shack**

Ms. X listened. Then she said, "Go to Task status." She would skim through the student summaries later.

Task status

• **Task 1: Finished. The team has finished Task 1. They found fresh air, food, clean water, and shelter.**
• **Madagascar: Team to depart. The Quest team will depart.** They will escape the K-T extinction.

Ms. X nodded and thought, "Good. The Quest 2300 team is following directions and moving forward." ***Beelzebufo* was sitting next to her foot. He had eaten and then hopped to the den. She said to him, "It appears that our team is doing**

well." Ms. X was glad to have her pet back. •• Where had *Beelzebufo* been?

To the left of the big screen were two smaller monitors. **A Quest logo and the words "Quest 2100" were on one of the screens.** Ms. X touched the screen. The photos of four world leaders flashed by.

Milly Masters	Prime Minister of Canada
Juliette Marceau	Nobel Peace Prize, Secretary General of the United Nations
Sergio Fedorov	Olympic Gold Medalist Track and Field
Kayaba Brown	Nobel Prize in Physics Robotics Engineer

Ms. X stared at the 2100 team. **Then she looked at the next screen. The Quest logo and "Quest 2200" appeared.** Ms. X sighed and touched the screen. **A team of six teens appeared. They had on baseball caps. Ms. X muttered to herself.** "And just one returned, just one, and no one knew." •• How many of the 2200 team members returned? •• What happened to the others?

Flashback to Quest 2200 • A loud sound, a crash! There was panic on the team. Darkness, yelling — then nothing.

Flashback to 2250 • A deep sleep. There had been silence for a long time. **A woman appeared out of nowhere.** She sat in a field of flowers. **She squinted at the sun. A horse stood near her, eating grass. She looked around for her team.** •• Who is the woman? •• What questions do you have?

The computer broke the quiet. "It is 7:00." Ms. X shook her head. **Then she petted the frog's armored back. Ms. X said out loud, "The 2300 team is a good team. I am confident of the outcome. *This* team will finish.** They will return to greatness." •• Do you think Ms. X is right? •• What do you think is going to happen to the Quest 2300 team?

The *Beelzebufo* **blinked and went back to sleep. Ms. X looked at the frog and thought, "When the 2300 team comes back, it will be bittersweet." With that, she transported herself to her classroom.** •• As used in the sentence, what does "bittersweet" mean? •• Why would the return of the 2300 team be bittersweet?

CHAPTER THIRTEEN

Mass Extinctions

Informational

Previously Learned

About 66 million years ago, a massive asteroid struck Earth. That is a fact. Scientists agree that the crash of a massive asteroid sent Earth into a mass extinction. There is a mountain of evidence that supports this hypothesis.

•• What is the evidence?

The catastrophic effect of the asteroid strike is widely accepted. **About 3 out of 4 plant and animal species went extinct.** There is also evidence that massive volcanic activity was part of this mass extinction.

Mass Extinction

What is a mass extinction? A mass extinction happens when:

- More than half of Earth's species vanish or go extinct.
- The extinction happens in a short period of time.

The K-T extinction occurred across 32,000 years. **Earth's history spans 4.6 billion years.** Scientists consider 32,000 years a short period of time. •• How old is the Earth? •• Why do scientists think 32,000 years is a short period of time?

Five Mass Extinctions

There have been five mass extinctions in Earth's long history. **The extinction that killed off the dinosaurs is just one. It is called the K-T extinction.** The K-T extinction is simply the most recent and the most talked about. •• Why do we know about the K-T extinction?

Look at the timeline below. The dots show when the mass extinctions occurred. •• **Count the dots. Find the K-T extinction. It is the fifth dot.**

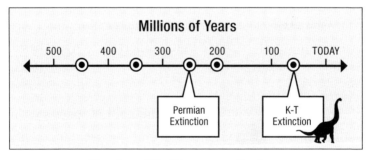

Timeline of Earth's mass extinctions

The Biggest Extinction in Earth's History

The biggest mass extinction of all happened long before the dinosaurs vanished from Earth. The Permian extinction occurred about 252 million years ago. **This extinction is called "The Great Dying."**

Look at the timeline again. The biggest extinction was the third mass extinction. •• **Count the dots. Put your finger on the biggest extinction.**

During the Permian extinction, about 90% of all species died out. This means that 9 out of ten plant and animal species went extinct. Nearly all living things vanished.

The Permian Period

What was Earth like before "The Great Dying?" During the Permian period, Pangea had already formed. Pangea was surrounded by a vast sea. Fossil evidence tells of coral reefs. There were fish and sharks. There were sponges and rays.

From coal deposits, scientists know that some parts of Pangea may have been a lot like today's tropical rainforests. There were mossy plants and the beginnings of Earth's evergreen forests.

The swampy forests were populated by the ancestors of reptiles, dinosaurs, and mammals. There were many living

By Phil Degginger/Carnegie Museum/Science Source

Landscape during the Permian Period

things. Insects were evolving. There were huge dragonflies. **Beetles had appeared.** •• Describe Pangea in the Permian Period.

Then something happened. There is evidence that almost all living things disappeared from Earth. •• What questions do you have about the Permian extinction? •• Do you have a hypothesis about what caused the mass extinction?

CHAPTER FOURTEEN

The Great Dying
Informational

Previously Learned

Earth is 4.6 billion years old. During that time, more than half of Earth's species have gone extinct. Mass extinctions have taken place not once or twice, but five times. **The biggest of all the mass extinctions was the Permian extinction. It happened 252 million years ago. ••** What hypotheses might explain why 90% of all species died out?

The Scientific Method •• What is the topic of this section? **As with all questions about Earth, scientists observe, ask questions, form hypotheses, and test their hypotheses.** Then, from this process, they draw conclusions.

Observations. Scientists can tell a story about an event that happened 252 million years ago. Plant and animal species were abundant. **Then they disappeared. Scientists can tell us that 9 out of ten species vanished from Earth.**

Questions. Scientists have asked, "What happened? What killed off almost all living things?" •• What important questions are scientists trying to answer?

Hypotheses. Scientists have formed best guesses. 1) An asteroid struck Earth. 2) Massive volcanic activity poured toxic gases into the air and damaged the Earth's atmosphere. 3) Climate change was the culprit.

Tests. It is difficult to test what happened 252 million years ago, but scientists keep looking for evidence. Scientists persevere. They keep looking for a mountain of evidence to prove what happened. •• Why do scientists have to persevere?

Conclusions. For years, some scientists thought an asteroid was the culprit in the Permian extinction. No one has found the smoking gun. No crater has been found. This hypothesis has not passed the test. •• Was an asteroid the cause of the Permian extinction?

The Culprit

In 2013, scientists hypothesized that the Permian extinction was the result of massive volcanic eruptions in Siberia. •• What was the hypothesis?

By 2015, scientists had concluded that huge lava flows from volcanic eruptions were definitely connected with the largest mass extinction in Earth's history.

Let's look at the test. Ancient rock cliffs were found in remote areas of Siberia. Scientists traveled there. •• Look at the map. Find Siberia.

Scientists found the following facts in the rocks:

Fact 1. The volcanoes erupted before the Permian extinction. They continued erupting during the extinction and for a short time after the mass extinction.

Fact 2. The eruptions lasted across 900,000 years.

Fact 3. The volcanic activity would have covered an area as large as the United States. (It is hard to imagine the amount of volcanic activity that took place in Pangea.) •• What facts did scientists learn from studying the Siberian rocks?

Computer models show how devastating the effects of the massive volcanic eruptions would have been. Toxic gases would have damaged layers of Earth's atmosphere. Without protection from the atmosphere, the sun would have warmed the Earth. **This would have resulted in hotter air and hotter sea water. Plants and animals could not adapt.**

Tiny organisms in the oceans died. The food chain was disrupted. **More and more animals were left without food.** The hotter temperatures resulted in "The Great Dying." •• Describe how the volcanic eruptions caused the Great Dying.

The Role of Science

By studying the rocks, scientists learn about Earth's history. They observe. They ask questions. They hypothesize. They

test for facts. They persevere! Finally, scientists draw conclusions based on a mountain of evidence.

By learning about Earth's history, scientists help us understand what has happened and what could happen. What will happen in the next hundred years? The next thousand years? And even the next million years? Evidence from the past can help people learn about the future. •• What can science help people do? •• What questions do you have?

CHAPTER FIFTEEN

Age of Mammals: The Giants

Informational

Today, scientists agree that an asteroid struck Earth about 66 million years ago. The crash killed living things and triggered massive volcanic activity. Animals that survived lost their food supply as the planet was plunged into darkness and then into global warming. **The K-T extinction took 32,000 years.** •• How long did the K-T extinction take?

Mammals

Not all animals were killed. Some small mammals lived. Some survived by burrowing underground to escape the extreme heat. **Other mammals moved into nearby waters.**

Across years, Earth began to cool. As Earth's surface cooled, the surviving mammals emerged in search of food. **The vast continent was barren, but the mammals still had a food supply. They could eat insects and plants that lived in the water. Mammals adapted.** •• What made it possible for some mammals to survive?

Mammals didn't just survive. **Across millions of years, mammal species increased.** Mammals began to rule Earth.

The Giants

With the plant-eating dinosaurs gone, the mammals had more to eat. Some small mammals evolved into bigger and bigger animals. In fact, some mammals evolved into giants.

•• Why were mammals able to evolve into giants?

By studying fossils and layers of rocks, scientists observed that the giant mammals reached their largest size 40 million years ago. Then, by about 10,000 years ago, most of the giant mammals had vanished. •• What questions do you have about the giant mammals?

A Giant in the Horse Family

A relative of today's horse, the Indricotherium (in-druh-koh-thār-EE-um) grew in size to about 20 tons (as heavy as ten cars). This giant stood about 18 feet tall. It lived 30 million years ago. This plant eater was the biggest of the land mammals. It was the king of the giant land mammals. This animal went extinct about 16 million years ago. •• Describe the king of the land animals.

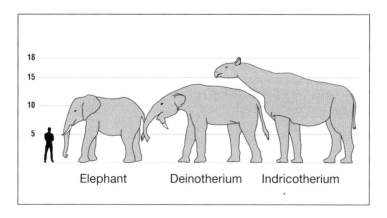

Elephant Family

Deinotherium (die-no-thār-EE-um) lived 23 million years ago. Our modern-day elephant is a descendant of this mammal. **This mammal stood about 15 feet tall. It went extinct about 1.8 million years ago.**

The mammoth is another relative of the elephant. **Across millions of years, mammoths moved across the land from Africa. One species, the woolly mammoth, traveled to the freezing cold lands of the north.** •• What did the woolly mammoth do?

Woolly mammoth

To keep warm, the mammoth developed long, shaggy fur. Under the fur, the big animals developed thick fat to help protect them from the cold. •• How did the mammoth adapt to the cold?

Woolly mammoths lived 400,000 years ago. Then around 10,000 years ago, most of them went extinct. •• Why do you think the mammoths went extinct?

Scientists are studying why many of the giant mammals disappeared about 10,000 years ago. They use the scientific **method to find answers.** •• How do scientists solve mysteries?

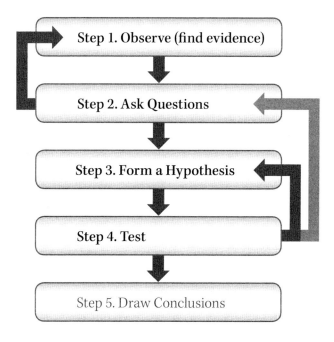

Step 1. Observe (find evidence)

Step 2. Ask Questions

Step 3. Form a Hypothesis

Step 4. Test

Step 5. Draw Conclusions

•• What do the arrows mean?

The End of the Giant Mammals

Step 1. Observe: Scientists observed that many of the giant mammals went extinct about 10,000 years ago.

Step 2. Ask Questions: Scientists asked, "What killed off the giant mammals 10,000 years ago?" •• What questions do you have?

Step 3. Form a Hypothesis: Scientists formed a hypothesis. Humans hunted giant mammals to extinction.

Step 4. Test: Scientists looked at fossils. They looked for evidence that the giant mammals had been hunted. Out of 36 giant mammal extinctions, they found evidence that just two of the species were hunted.

Step 5. Draw Conclusions: Human hunting may have played a part in the extinction of two giant mammals, but it is not the reason many species died out at the same time. •• Look at the chart on the previous page. Work through the steps of the scientific method. Explain what scientists did at each step to determine that hunting was not the cause of most giant mammal extinctions.

When a hypothesis is not proven, what do scientists do? They keep digging into the past. They look for more facts. •• Do scientists persevere? How?

Step 2. Ask more questions. Scientists asked more questions. Could the extinctions have to do with the planet getting hotter and colder?

Step 3. Form another hypothesis. Most giant mammals went extinct due to climate change.

Step 4. Run more tests. By 2014, scientists had studied warming events across millions of years. They found that giant mammals went extinct when Earth got hotter. When the climate suddenly got warmer, the giant mammals vanished.

Conclusion: **Scientists agree.** Rapid warming events contributed to the demise of the giant mammals. •• What did scientists conclude?

CHAPTER SIXTEEN

Moving Forward
Narrative Fiction

Previously in the Third Quest

The team had found a cave, a stream, and dinosaur eggs. Shack said, "We did it. We got shelter. We got good fresh air, clean water, and we got food."

Then, in the a blink of an eye, everything had changed. The air was so cold Shack could see his breath. **It was bitterly cold. ••** What do you think happened? •• What text evidence supports your conclusion?

• • •

Shack said to himself, "Look cool. Act cool. Be cool."

Then he shook himself and yelled. "Hey."

"Hey back," Mindy said. Then she looked around and counted. All six team members were accounted for.

Anna asked, "What's going on?"

Shack said, "Zoom, zoom, zoom."

Ling said, "We have traveled somewhere again."

Mindy looked at Zack, but he said nothing.

Shack looked at Tuppins. **"Hey, kid. What is going on? Where are we?"**

Tuppins grinned and began talking. "Given the change in climate, it would appear that we have been transported from the time of the K-T extinction. It's rather unfortunate, as the opportunity to meet up with a living dinosaur has no doubt passed." •• What makes Tuppins think they had been transported? •• Why is he disappointed?

The others were thinking, "It's better not to be extinct."

Shack said, "It's good. We didn't get killed. We left the dying dinosaurs and Madagascar. So Tuppins, where are we? We need relevant info." •• What do they need?

Tuppins seemed puzzled. Anna pointed to a fire pit. There were coals and a few bones.

Tuppins looked and started talking again. "It would appear that we are in the Age of Mammals. **Mammals began to appear on Earth about 200 million years ago.** When the dinosaurs went extinct, many new mammals began to appear. Actually, it wasn't just mammals. After the demise of the dinosaurs, new species of flowering plants, insects, fish, and bird species gradually appeared."

Shack was remembering what Ms. X had said. You are lucky. Tuppins will go with you. You will all be happy that he is with you. •• What evidence suggests that Tuppins is an asset?

Anna said, "Look, it's another folder."

To: The Travelers
From: Quest Central
Date: The year 2300
Subject: Quest 2300

Task 1. Find air, food, clean water, and shelter.
- **Did you find fresh air? Yes.**
- **Did you find food? Yes.**
- **Did you find clean water? Yes.**
- **Did you find shelter? Yes.**

Congratulations. You followed the rules and completed Task 1. Your reward: You have each been given a Zero Suit to protect you from the extreme cold. You will still need to meet your basic needs throughout the Quest.

Task 2. Follow the clues. The first clue is Yuka (YOO-kuh).

Good luck.

•• How was the team successful? •• What was their reward? •• Do you think the clue "Yuka" is relevant? Why? •• What does the team need to do next?

Ling looked into the pit and said, "Tuppins, do you remember studying Yuka?"

Shack looked at Ling and said, " Yuka. What is Yuka?"

Ling said, "Yuka was a baby mammoth. She lived 40,000 years ago in Siberia. We must be in Siberia."

Mindy said. "That's good. We are going forward in time."

Ling said, "Not so good. All humans were nomads 40,000 years ago. They hunted for food. That fire pit was made by humans. If humans are around, they will not be friendly."

•• What is Ling worried about? •• Is Ling an asset? •• Find information in the text to support your answer.

Shack said, "So, we need to be cautious in case an unfriendly human shows up." Ling nodded.

Mindy looked around at the team. She thought, "We are all in this together. Ling and Tuppins know a lot about history. Shack will be bold, but he will also follow directions. Anna is great. She is observant and will take action." Then Mindy looked at Zack. He was standing off to the side. Mindy thought, "He is still not himself." •• What makes Ling and Tuppins assets? •• What makes Anna a strong team member? •• Why is Mindy unsure about Zack?

Tuppins began talking again. "Yuka was killed by a big animal. They believe it was a cave lion." •• What do you think will happen next?

The Clue: Yuka

Narrative Fiction

Previously in the Third Quest

The team had been transported. They found themselves **in another cave.** A new memo had appeared. The kids were rewarded with Zero Suits to keep them warm. A new clue was given — "Yuka." **Yuka was a baby mammoth that had lived in Siberia 40,000 years ago. This told the team they were in Siberia 40,000 years in the past.** They would still need to watch for their basic needs. •• What are the four basic needs?

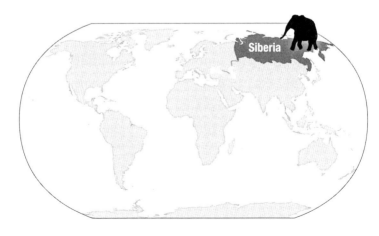

Siberia

● ● ●

Mindy was still curious about the clue "Yuka." She said, "Tuppins, what else do you know about Yuka?"

Tuppins grinned at the request. Then he launched into a new soliloquy. **"In 2010, tusk hunters found Yuka. The tusk hunters lived in northern Siberia.** These people braved harsh conditions to search for the huge mammoth tusks. The tusks were sold for thousands of dollars."

Anna said, "That's interesting, Tuppins, but I don't think it's relevant." •• Why is the information on tusk hunting not relevant?

Ling said, "We need to think about food and water."

Tuppins wasn't really listening to anyone. He just kept talking. "In the early 2000s, there were warming temperatures. Ground that had been frozen for thousands of years began melting. The melting ice revealed mammoth tusks and bones. Tusk traders hoped to find great wealth. A tusk weighs about 100 pounds. **The tusks were sold for $400 a pound."**

Shack looked at Tuppins. "Too cool. If we can find a tusk or two, that would be 40 to 80 thousand dollars. Think about it! Three tusks would be $120,000!"

Mindy looked at Tuppins and Shack, and then said calmly, "Tuppins and Shack, we need to focus. We have 40,000 years to travel through." •• Why does Mindy tell Tuppins and Shack to focus? •• What is most important: getting rich, following the clue "Yuka," or finding food?

Shack stopped and grinned at Mindy. He remembered he was hungry. He said, "We do need food."

Anna said, "Look, there's another folder." She picked it up and began reading the memo.

To: The Travelers
From: Quest Central
Date: **The year 2300**
Subject: **Focus**

Task 1. Do not forget. Your basic needs are important. Your survival will always depend on meeting your basic needs.

Task 2. Follow the clues. You figured out the clue "Yuka." **You are in Siberia 40,000 years ago. It is important to focus.** Do not get sidetracked. The clue "Yuka" is still relevant. Continue thinking about Yuka. Focus on the circumstances of her early death. •• What is relevant?

Anna said, "It's kind of creepy. The people who set up the Quest must be listening to us." •• What is creepy?

Tuppins started talking again. "Scientists hypothesized that Yuka was attacked by a cave lion. She had unhealed bites and a broken leg. **She also had a long cut across her back. Scientists think a lion attacked Yuka. Then humans took over, but her body was still intact.** Scientists don't know why the humans left her body behind."

Anna said, "Do we need to hunt mammoths for food? Is that what the clue means? **Has anyone ever hunted?**"

Shack said, "Not me."

Mindy said, "**Our robot brings us food.** If 'Yuka' means we have to hunt for our food, then we are in trouble. **We don't have anything to hunt with.** Maybe we can find plants to eat."

Ling said, "Maybe the clue has to do with the cave lion killing Yuka." There was silence. **Perhaps they would be the lion's next meal. The kids peered deep into the darkness of the cave.** Three pairs of eyes stared back at the kids. •• Who or what is in the cave? •• What do you think will happen next?

CHAPTER EIGHTEEN

Lyuba

Informational

In May 2007, a reindeer herder stood on a sandbar in a river in northern Siberia. He and his sons had found the body of a small mammoth — a baby mammoth. Mammoths had been extinct in Siberia for 10,000 years, yet this body was intact. The reindeer herder had seen mammoth tusks before, but never the body of a mammoth. •• When did the reindeer herders find the baby mammoth? •• Why do you think they found the body in the late spring?

The mammoth body had been encased in ice for thousands of years, but the ice had begun to melt. **The reindeer herder and his sons could see the animal's preserved fur, body, trunk, and four legs.** They could even see the animal's tail. •• What do you think was unusual about the body?

The herders did not touch the baby mammoth. **They believed mammoths walked in the underworld. The herders thought the mammoth could be a bad omen. The herders left the baby mammoth behind and traveled to ask a friend what to do. The body must be an important find.** •• Why did the herders leave the baby mammoth behind? (Use information from the text to support your answer.)

The men went to the director of a small town museum. The director was so excited he persuaded authorities to fly a helicopter to the baby mammoth. **When the helicopter landed, the baby mammoth was gone. Just as she had appeared, she had suddenly vanished. Or had she? Had someone stumbled across her body? Did someone steal her? If so, who was the culprit?**

The herder learned that his cousin had taken the baby mammoth and sold it for two snowmobiles and a year's worth of food. •• Why did the cousin take the baby mammoth?

The baby mammoth was found leaning on the wall of a store. The baby mammoth stood about 4 feet tall. She was still intact, but a dog had gnawed on her tail and ear. With the help of the police, the ancient creature was returned to the herder. The baby mammoth was taken by helicopter to a museum near the Arctic Circle. She was named Lyuba after the herder's wife. **Lyuba means love.**

The baby
mammoth
Lyuba

By James St. John (CC BY 2.0)

The helicopter trip was the start of a long but important journey for baby Lyuba. **Better than the fossils of an extinct animal, Lyuba's body was perfectly preserved.** •• What does "Lyuba's body was preserved" mean?

There would be a lot to learn from Lyuba. Scientists from around the world had many questions. In fact, Lyuba has been studied by scientists from all over the world. •• Why was the discovery of Lyuba's body important? •• If you were a scientist, what questions would you have about Lyuba?

Today, Lyuba is part of a woolly mammoth exhibit. Her home is still in Siberia. Russia lends Lyuba to museums in other countries. **The baby mammoth is on display around the world. She may even visit where you live. People can also see models of Lyuba. At 40,000 years old, Lyuba is a star.** •• If Lyuba came to a museum near you, would you go? Why?

CHAPTER NINETEEN

Studying Lyuba

Informational

By James St. John (CC BY 2.0)

Scientists were excited to hear about Lyuba. **Scientists from all over the world wanted to study the baby mammoth.** A scientist from the United States, Dr. Dan Fisher, had spent 30 years studying mammoth fossils.

Even before Lyuba was found, Dr. Fisher asked many questions about woolly mammoths. Humans had hunted

mammoths for thousands of years. Dr. Fisher wondered how human hunters had stored mammoth meat. The massive animals would be worth hunting only if the meat could be preserved. •• Why would the meat need to be preserved?

Dr. Fisher ran a test. He butchered a work horse with stone tools. **Then he stored the meat in a pond. The meat became pickled.** Fisher ate the slightly sour-smelling meat every two weeks from February until summer. •• A conclusion: A character trait of Dr. Fisher is curiosity. What did he do that supports this conclusion?

Lyuba, the First Studies

Dr. Fisher was one of the first scientists to study Lyuba. He was invited to Russia to study the baby mammoth. This was an honor. Dr. Fisher was very excited.

Observation

The body was nearly perfect. The scientist could even see Lyuba's eyelashes. Lyuba had not been attacked by another animal. She had not been hunted and killed by human hunters. •• What questions do you have?

Question

The scientists asked, "How did Lyuba die?"

Hypotheses

Scientists thought she may have been ill or had no food to eat.

Tests
- **Test 1:** Samples of Lyuba's body were sent away to be dated. **The tests revealed that she lived about 40,000 years ago.** •• How old was Lyuba's body?
- **Test 2: About six months after Lyuba's body was found, she was sent to Japan.** A CT scan revealed that her skeleton was not damaged and her internal organs were healthy. There were no signs of illness or poor health.

Conclusion

Scientists believed it was unlikely that Lyuba died from starvation or illness. •• What questions do you have now?

Lyuba, the Next Studies

In 2008, Dr. Fisher returned to Russia. **There, he and other scientists from around the world began another set of tests.** This time, they would use surgical procedures to learn more about Lyuba. **They would study her ears, teeth, fat, and organs.**

Scientists found a healthy baby mammoth. There were still no signs of starvation or illness. **Scientists did find that Lyuba's trunk, mouth, and lungs were filled with a mix of clay and sand.** •• What conclusions would you draw from this evidence?

Conclusion

Scientists concluded that baby Lyuba had indeed suffocated. **They think Lyuba stumbled on a slippery riverbank and** was dragged into mud. In her panic, they think the small mammoth sucked mud into her mouth, trunk, and lungs. •• Does this verify what you were thinking?

Another Question

The scientists wondered, "How was it possible for the body to be fully preserved after 40,000 years?"

Observations and Tests

During the 2008 investigation, the international team of scientists allowed Lyuba's body to thaw. **They had to work quickly so Lyuba's body would not rot. Dr. Fisher observed an odd smell coming from the body.** It was the same smell that Dr. Fisher had noticed when he ate the pickled horse meat! •• What conclusion can you draw from the information in the text?

Drawing Conclusions

Scientists have concluded that Lyuba's body was preserved through a pickling process. **The pickling prevented her body from rotting.**

Question

Could humans have preserved meat in ponds 40,000 years ago? •• What do you think?

Lyuba's early demise was sad, but she is a star 40,000 years after she was born. •• What have we learned from Lyuba?

CHAPTER TWENTY

Humans

Narrative Fiction

Previously in the Third Quest

The team was in a cave in the cold arctic lands of Siberia. It was 40,000 years ago.

The clue "Yuka" was still relevant. **The baby mammoth had been killed by a cave lion. A long cut across her back had been made by humans.**

• • •

Dim light from the Arctic sun seeped into the cave. The kids could see six eyes glaring at them. **Before they could act, Shack hissed, "Do not run. Freeze."** •• What do you think is in the cave?

A fire pit lay between some big cats and the team. Zack leaned into the pit. Flames jumped up as Zack stepped back. •• What danger does the team face? •• Which team members took charge, and how?

The kids slowly backed out of the cave. **The mother cat stayed with her cubs. The team began walking across the barren landscape.**

Finally, Mindy yelled, "Do we just keep walking?"

Anna hollered, "We need to talk!" The six kids huddled together. •• It says the kids huddled together. What does it mean to "huddle"?

Shack looked at Tuppins and said, "Hey, kid, tell us something important."

Tuppins said, "Humans were hunter-gatherers. They were nomads. They followed animals like the woolly mammoths and reindeer." Then Tuppins started talking about preserving meat and bacteria in ponds. Before he could finish a soliloquy on food preservation, Ling interrupted.

Ling said, "This is what's relevant. Humans made spears and hunted for meat. They will not be friendly, but they do know how to survive here." •• Describe how humans lived 40,000 years ago.

Shack said, "So, where there are humans, there is food. We got to keep moving."

As they trudged across the frozen land, the team could see cliffs looming ahead. Hours later, they found an opening in the rocks — another cave. Anna threw a pebble into the cave. **Nothing happened. The kids entered.** •• Why does Anna toss a pebble into the cave? •• Describe Anna.

A muffled cry came from deep in the cave. A baby? Another lion's cub? They stood very still. Finally, Shack crept deeper into the cave. Soon he motioned for the others to follow. The cave looked abandoned, but there was a pile of berries and dried meat in a corner.

The kids forgot about the cry. They were hungry. Anna divided the berries and meaty-looking stuff among the team members. A small stream ran along the cave wall. They had found food, shelter, and water again.

Anna put her fingers to her lips. "Shhh." There was the sound again. It was a human baby crying.

Tuppins walked deeper into the cave. A human mother and her baby crouched in a corner. Tuppins whispered, "I'm friendly. It's okay." The human didn't understand. She picked up a rock. •• Why does the human pick up a rock?

Shack grabbed Tuppins. "It isn't safe to stay. When their clan gets back . . . " Tuppins nodded. There was no way to communicate with the humans. •• Why would it be dangerous for the team to meet up with the humans?

The team walked along the cliffs, hidden from sight. But Mindy stumbled on something soft and squishy. A big frog was sitting at her feet on a red folder. Without thinking, Mindy picked up the *Beelzebufo*. Anna grabbed the folder and began reading.

To: The Travelers
From: Quest Central
Date: The year 2300
Subject: Traveler's Reward

Congratulations. You followed the rules and completed Task 2. Your reward: One of you may go home. Who will it be? It is up to you. You have five minutes to determine your fate. Good luck.

•• What is the reward? •• Who do you think will go home?

Shack said, "I will stay and Tuppins needs to stay, too."

•• Why does Shack offer to stay?

Ling said, "I'm in. Tuppins and I go way back. I can translate his soliloquies."

Anna said, "I'm staying, too. This is better than the decrepit school."

Next, Mindy said, "The frog is a good omen. I'm in, too. Zack, I guess you get to go home."

Zack showed little emotion. Mindy thought again, "He reminds me of my robot." But Zack said, "I'll stay." Then he muttered, "There's no reason to go back." •• Why do you think Zack is acting aloof? •• Which team members chose to stay?

Mindy started to ask Zack what he meant, but she found herself on a hot, dusty street with the rest of the team. The *Beelzebufo* was riding in a sling around her shoulder. •• Listen to me read that paragraph again, and then name two things that are absurd.

CHAPTER TWENTY-ONE

The Woolly Mammoths of St. Paul Island

Informational

Introduction

The woolly mammoth went extinct in North America, Asia, and Europe about 10,000 years ago. •• Where did the woolly mammoth live? •• When did they go extinct?

Most scientists agree that the woolly mammoths went extinct because of climate warming, a shrinking food supply, and human hunting. •• Why did they go extinct?

A small population of woolly mammoths survived about five thousand years longer. **The St. Paul woolly mammoths lived on a small Alaskan island. Then they also went extinct.** •• What questions do you think the scientists asked?

Topic 1. An Island Habitat

How did the woolly mammoths end up on St. Paul Island? **For thousands of years, woolly mammoths migrated from Asia to North America.** They crossed a narrow land bridge that connected the two continents. Look at the drawing of Earth.

The dotted line shows the land bridge from Asia to North America.

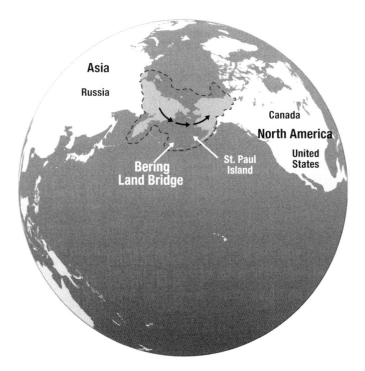

Bering land bridge, woolly mammoth crossing

Then, about 11,000 years ago, the climate warmed. Glaciers melted, and rising sea waters slowly flooded the land bridge.

The woolly mammoths did not know that seawater was beginning to surround the land. The mammoths kept moving to higher ground. **With seawater all around them, they could not leave.** The mammoths became stranded on a newly formed island. •• How were the woolly mammoths stranded?

Topic 2. An Extinction Mystery

For thousands of years, the woolly mammoths did well on St. Paul Island. Then, 5,600 years ago, they also went extinct. For years, scientists have asked what killed off the woolly mammoths of St. Paul Island.

- Did human hunters kill off the mammoths?
- Did volcanic activity kill off the mammoths?
- Were they killed off by predators?
- Did climate warming kill off the mammals?
•• Which hypothesis do you think is most likely?

The first hypothesis was easy to rule out. There is no evidence of humans on the island until about 300 years ago. That means the woolly mammoths were extinct by the time humans arrived. Clearly, humans did not kill off the woolly mammoths of St. Paul Island.

The second hypothesis was also ruled out. There is no evidence of volcanic activity during the time of extinction.

Scientists also quickly ruled out other predators. The only animals on the island during the time of the woolly mammoths were arctic foxes and small mouse-like mammals. Polar bears arrived about 1,500 years after the St. Paul mammoths went extinct. •• Scientists ruled out three hypotheses. What were they?

Topic 3. Climate Warming

With climate warming, St. Paul Island kept shrinking. With less land and less plant life, scientists thought the woolly mammoths lacked food. Their hypothesis: Climate warming caused the woolly mammoths to starve to death.

In 2013, scientists traveled to St. Paul Island to test their hypothesis and answer questions. They asked, "When did the woolly mammoths of St. Paul Island go extinct? What changes in the habitat resulted in their demise? Was there enough food for the woolly mammoths?" The answer stunned the scientists. •• What do you think the word "stunned" means as used in the last sentence?

CHAPTER TWENTY-TWO

Mystery Solved

Informational

Scientists from around the world work together. They pool their knowledge and skills to answer complex questions.
•• What do scientists from around the world do?

In 2016, a team of scientists traveled to St. Paul Island. The team braved the freezing cold to gather samples of earth from deep under a freshwater lake.

The samples were sent to labs in Canada and the United States. Scientists studied ancient remains of:

- Mammoth DNA
- Pollen
- Volcanic ash
- Plant life
- Water fleas
- Fungus

•• From the samples of earth, what did the scientists study?

From mammoth DNA and the fungus that grows on mammoth dung, scientists learned that the last woolly mammoths disappeared 5,600 years ago. **Modern-day methods made it possible for scientists to date when the mammoths** went extinct within 100 years. •• What did scientists learn from the mammoth DNA?

They asked, "What happened 5,600 years ago? What was the culprit?"

Tests revealed that food was not a problem when the mammoths went extinct. Water fleas and plant pollens had not changed when the mammals went extinct. The animals did not starve to death. •• How did scientists know food was not a problem for the woolly mammoths?

Tests revealed that a rise in sea level had made the groundwater salty. There was also less rainwater at the time the mammoths died out. The two freshwater lakes on the island had become shallower. •• What might scientists now think was the problem?

Based on modern-day elephants, scientists estimate a woolly mammoth needed 70 to 100 gallons of fresh water per day. There is evidence that the mammoths trampled the lake shores trying to get water. The lake water became cloudy, and their freshwater supply shrank even more. •• What happened to the lake water?

Conclusion

Why did the mammoths of St. Paul Island go extinct? What was the culprit? From a preponderance of evidence, scientists have concluded that the St. Paul Island mammoths went extinct due to a lack of fresh water. They died of thirst. Scientists see a lesson for the modern day. When the climate warms, fresh water is at risk. The lack of fresh water can drive extinction. •• What was the important thing scientists learned?

Informational Text

The story of the St. Paul woolly mammoths is informational. •• When you read informational text, what do you think the author's purpose is?

1. to tell a story
2. to make you cry
3. to provide information
4. to get a laugh

From extinction evidence, scientists keep learning more about Earth. •• What did you learn from the extinction of the St. Paul Island mammoths?

CHAPTER TWENTY-THREE

The Third Challenge

Narrative Fiction

Previously in the Third Quest

The Important When and Where: The team had been transported to Siberia 40,000 years ago. •• Where is Siberia?

The Important What: The team had followed the rules, seen a human mother and her baby, and completed Task 2. The Quest memo said a team member could return to 2300. Everyone on the team chose to stay. Suddenly the team was transported, but where?

• • •

The Important When: The year 2300
The Important Where: The decrepit school

Blurry images streamed into the room. The holograms were barely visible in Ms. X's decrepit classroom. The class could see ghost-like people milling around them.

Ms. X stood with her hands on her hips. The class was looking intently at the holograms. No one said a thing. One team member was coming back. •• Picture or visualize what the team members look like. Describe the holograms.

Ms. X said, "So, someone will be back. Who do you think it will be? Mindy? Zack? Who? The team is still deciding who will come back to the year 2300." •• You know the answer, but the class doesn't. Who is coming back?

Shack's best friend predicted, "Shack won't leave the team. He has integrity. Shack will stay." •• Why will Shack stay?

Shack's face appeared from inside the Siberian cave. He flashed a big grin. The class could hear him say boldly, "Tuppins and I are in."

The images in the classroom swirled — flashing too fast to follow. All of a sudden, the setting changed. The travelers were on a dusty street. Mindy appeared. She was in a long dress. Ms. X looked surprised. She mumbled, "So, the girl from the Hill stayed, too." •• What in the text leads you to believe the travelers have left Siberia? •• Why do you think Ms. X is surprised that Mindy stayed?

The images disappeared, and a picture appeared on the wall. The class could see all six of the Quest travelers. Ms. X nodded. She seemed pleased. The team was intact. Shack, Tuppins, Ling, Anna, and Zack had been expected to stay.

The test had been for Mindy. Mindy didn't ask for things, but her parents gave her the best of everything. •• Do you think Mindy is spoiled? Why or why not?

Suddenly the live feed stopped. Ms. X looked intently at a glass wall. Her thoughts appeared on the glass. She had transmitted a question and the words were on display.

Why did everyone stay?

There was a buzz in the class. Someone whispered, "Ms. X has an implant."

Another kid said, "Why would they give an old, decrepit teacher an implant?" •• In this passage, what do you think the word "implant" means?

Someone whispered, "Droid. Maybe she is an android." •• Why does the student think Ms. X is an android?

Ms. X turned and glared at the wall. Then she said quietly, "Enough. One of your classmates could have returned, but they all stayed. Why? Melvin, you said Shack stayed because he has integrity. What do you mean by that?"

Melvin hesitated but said, "Shack is responsible. He never lets us down. He does what's right."

Ms. X nodded. "Shack is an asset. He is bold but not a fool. What about the others? Comforts have been removed. Why did they stay? Speak up." •• Why do you think everyone on the team stayed?

The class was quiet. No one said anything. Ms. X waited. Finally, a hand went up. Ms. X said, "First, tell me your name. Then tell me what you think."

"My name is Kate. No one could leave the team, not really. No one would abandon the others." Then she said, "The offer was kind of mean. Why did Quest try to mess up the team?" •• In this paragraph, what does "abandon" mean?

Ms. X nodded and said, "That is good thinking. Perhaps you should be on the team." Then Ms. X said, "The team of six will continue going forward in time."

As was their habit, the kids were no longer paying attention, but Ms. X kept talking. She said, "Individually and collectively, the travelers will be asked to put forth their best efforts. Their survival will depend on each team member's ability to persevere and your ability to support their efforts." •• What did the team need for survival?

Ms. X left the classroom. On the glass display, she left the words:

> **Be prepared.**
> What is the Cradle of Civilization?
> **Lives may depend on the answer.**

Kate looked at the display and shivered. Then the bell rang, and the words vanished. Poof. •• What makes the chapter end on an ominous note?

CHAPTER TWENTY-FOUR

Lambert and Kate

Narrative Fiction

Previously in the Third Quest

The team had been given an opportunity to send one team member back to the year 2300, but no one wanted to leave the team. •• What traits have the travelers all demonstrated?

• • •

The Important When: The year 2300
The Important Where: Lambert's home

Lambert

Lambert couldn't quit thinking about the team. His computer had sensed him entering his room. Lambert sat at his desk.

Buster said, "Lambert. It is good to sense your presence. **I hope you had a great day."** •• Who is Buster? •• What in the text tells you that he's a computer?

Lambert said, "Hey, Buster. So, I've been thinking. Can you find a backdoor into Quest?"

Buster said, "I've been looking at the weekly reports. There are many websites reporting on the travelers. It sounds like the team has been moved forward in time. It is quite interesting. They are becoming stars. They've got millions of followers.

"People are concerned that the travelers were not prepared to survive in this environment. They do not have the needed skills."

Lambert just glared at Buster. Then Lambert asked again, "Can you find a backdoor into the Quest files?"

Buster was clearly unhappy. "No, sir! I cannot hack into the Quest computers! That's a criminal activity. Your teacher can log in whenever she wants." •• Why is Buster unhappy? •• Who do you think Lambert is?

Lambert said, "That's the problem — decrepit school, decrepit computer, cranky old teacher. Ms. X won't let us view the Quest team for more than a few minutes at a time." •• Why is Lambert upset?

Buster was distressed. "I could do it, but it is forbidden. I am not permitted to go in backdoors. Please do not ask." •• What in the text shows that Buster is an exceptional computer?

Lambert was thinking. "I should be on the Third Quest. There has to be a way in." He was glad Buster could not read his thoughts. •• Describe Lambert.

Kate

Kate walked slowly home through a decrepit neighborhood. (The decrepit school was in her neighborhood. It was the only school she knew.) She was thinking about Ms. X's message: **Be prepared.** What is the Cradle of Civilization? **Lives may depend on the answer.**

Their class would need to be prepared, but no one had paid attention to Ms. X's message, no one except Kate and maybe Lambert.

Kate began thinking, "Cradle of Civilization . . . Cradle of Civilization."

Kate sent her mom a text, "Going to the library." Their home computer would do her little good. She often couldn't log onto the Internet.

Her mom messaged back: "Be home for dinner."

Kate ran up the library steps and logged into the history computer — Homer. Password: Kate123. Then she stepped into a sound booth. •• Why does Kate go to the library?

Kate said, "Hi, Homer. I need your help. What can you tell me about the Cradle of Civilization?"

Homer said, "Greetings, Kate. What would you like to learn about the Cradle of Civilization?"

Kate said, "I don't know. **What is it? Where is it? Why is it called the Cradle of Civilization?**"

Homer said, "I will plot a research pathway for you. It will just be a second." •• Who or what do you think Homer is?

In a split second, Kate was walking through wheat fields. People were toiling in the fields — digging out canals and harvesting the wheat with sickles.

Kate blinked, thinking she had to be mistaken. But it was real. Kate thought, "Homer transported me." She looked at the people but felt very alone. Kate had no one to ask, so she asked herself, "Is this the Cradle of Civilization?" •• What happened to Kate?

Think about Kate at school. Think about her neighborhood and why she went to the library. •• What do you know about Kate?

CHAPTER TWENTY-FIVE

The Cradle of Civilization, Part 1

Informational

10,000 Years Ago

Ten thousand years ago, Earth was much as it is today. **Most people were hunter-gatherers. They migrated across the land in a never-ending quest for food.** They were nomads. •• Describe how people lived ten thousand years ago.

Gradually, some people learned they could gather wild plants, plant the seeds, and grow new plants. **These people were the first farmers. They tamed animals and began herding flocks of sheep.**

7,000 Years Ago, Mesopotamia

About 7,000 years ago, some people migrated to the land between the Tigris River and Euphrates River. This land was called Mesopotamia. **In Greek, the word "Mesopotamia" means "land between the rivers."** •• Turn the page and trace the Euphrates River and the Tigris River. •• What was the land between those rivers called?

Mesopotamia was desolate and barren. The early settlers of this region were called Sumerians. There was little rainfall.

However, the rivers flooded each year and made the land fertile. •• What do you think the word "fertile" means?

Accomplishments

The First Farmers

The Sumerians did not leave the barren land. They worked hard and learned to control the water. They built a system to water their crops and stop the flooding.

Their advanced irrigation systems required the hard work of many people. Their work would pay off. The Sumerians had more food than they could eat. •• Why did the Sumerians have more food than they could eat?

The First Cities

With farming, the Sumerians no longer had to wander in search of food. Farming led to another development — city life. Instead of migrating from place to place, people began living together. They had different jobs. They learned to make bricks from mud. They built homes. Two-story homes were built for the noblemen. Impressive temples were built for the gods. Walls were built to protect the people from other tribes. •• Why did the Sumerians develop city life? •• What kinds of jobs do you think they had?

The Wheel
With farming, some people weren't needed to gather and hunt for food. So people began inventing things. The Sumerians made pottery, and they learned to weave. About 5,500 years ago, the Sumerians also invented the wheel. First they invented the potter's wheel. Then, about three hundred years later, they began putting wheels on carts pulled by animals. •• Why was the wheel an important invention?

The First Writing and Number Systems
The Sumerians were also the first people to record things. In fact, the Sumerians were the first to invent a writing system and a number system. Writing and number systems gave the people a way to keep track of their goods, trades, and services. •• Why were the Sumerians impressive?

Way of Life
Religion
The Sumerians worshipped many gods and goddesses. Slaves, who were taken in war, built splendid temples. The people thought their gods lived in the temples and protected them from harm. •• Describe the Sumerians' religion. •• Who built the temples?

Ziggurat, Mesopotamian temple

Rulers

During times of war, Sumerians chose leaders who ruled until the war was over. Eventually these leaders became kings who ruled until death. Then power was handed over to their sons.

The Sumerian civilization lasted about 1,300 years. Then, about 4,000 years ago, the civilization ended. The land was invaded by a northern tribe, and the last king was taken captive. This great civilization was split up into many states. •• Why do you think the northern tribe was able to take over the Sumerians?

Mesopotamia Today

Mesopotamia was located in modern-day Iraq and Syria in a region referred to as the Middle East. **Today, the land between the two rivers is again barren, desolate, and torn by war. Look at the map. Find Syria and Iraq.**

Mesopotamia (dark gray) is located in today's Middle East.

Cradle of Civilization

Mesopotamia is called the Cradle of Civilization. Historians view Mesopotamia as the birthplace of civilization. •• Do you agree? What text in the chapter supports your opinion?

CHAPTER TWENTY-SIX

The Cradle of Civilization, Part 2

Informational

Previously Learned

For thousands of years, people were not civilized. They did not read or write. They had no science, no laws, and no governments. **They were nomads who lived by hunting, fishing, and gathering food. Then, about 7,000 years ago, a tribe of people migrated to Mesopotamia.**

Mesopotamia means the land between two rivers. The people were called the Sumerians. In what is now modern-day Iraq, the Sumerians developed the first farms. The first farms led to the world's first large cities. •• Describe how the first farms led to the first big cities.

The First Known Writing System

About 5,300 years ago, the Sumerians invented the first known writing system. **They wrote on clay and used reeds for pens. To write, the Sumerians pressed the reeds into wet clay. Then they baked the clay in the sun.**

Why did the Sumerians invent writing? The answer is farming. People needed a way to keep track of their crops, what was traded, and what was offered to the gods. Writing was developed so people could keep records. •• Why did the Sumerians develop writing?

The writing system evolved. At first, people made clay tokens for trade. Look at the picture. It shows tokens.

By Denise Schmandt-Besserat and the University of Pennsylvania Museum of Archaeolpolgy and Anthroplogy, University of Pennsylvania

Later, clay tablets were used to keep track of information. At first, the Sumerians wrote in pictures. Over time, the marks became more triangular and wedge shaped. •• How did writing evolve?

British Museum, London

The writing is called cuneiform. It was difficult to learn. **People who could read and write were called scribes.** Boys, and eventually girls, from wealthy families went to school to learn how to read and write. •• Who went to the schools? •• How do you think we know there were schools?

Perseverance: Unlocking the Code

Archaeologists found written records in the temples, tombs, and the remains of the ancient cities of Mesopotamia. **No one could read them because no one could speak Sumerian.**

Then, in the 1800s, ancient writing was found on a cliff wall. The writing told a story in three languages — one of which was cuneiform. By carefully comparing the stories, scholars were able to translate the cuneiform symbols. **Most of the code was broken in 1857.** For example, scholars found that:

$$\blacktriangleright\!\!\blacktriangleright\!\!\!— \; = A$$

•• Describe the process of breaking the code.

Prehistory and History

At first, the scribes used cuneiform to keep track of farm products bought and sold. **Later, they used writing to keep track of taxes and temple activities.** They wrote stories and letters, and schoolchildren even wrote journals. •• How do historians know about the life of schoolchildren?

With the invention of writing, we have history. We don't have to guess what people were thinking and doing. With writing, people from the past can speak to us.

The invention of writing separates prehistory from history. Prehistory is the time before events were written. Today we have a written history of the past. •• What is the difference between prehistory and history?

A big idea: All civilizations have a writing system. A written language allows scientists to share information and pass on knowledge. Without a written language, each generation would have to reinvent what we already know. •• Why is the ability to read and write a big deal?

CHAPTER TWENTY-SEVEN

A Silver Ribbon

Narrative Fiction

Previously in the Third Quest

Lambert wanted Buster to hack into the Quest computers. Buster said hacking was not permitted. •• Who is intrigued by the Quest? •• What makes you think so?

Ms. X left a note for the class. "What is the Cradle of Civilization? Lives may depend on the answer."

Kate was worried about the team. She went to the library, but was sent back in time by mistake. •• Do you think Kate wants to be there?

• • •

The Important When: The year 2300
The Important Where: Lambert's home

Lambert sat in his room, red with anger. He could see Kate's hologram. She was in Mesopotamia. Why Kate? It should have been him!

Buster said, "Lambert, it is good to sense your presence. I hope you had a great day." •• Who is Buster?

Lambert ignored Buster. He was angry with the computer. He was angry with Kate. He was angry with Ms. X, and he was angry with Quest. He should have been picked to be a traveler. •• How does Lambert feel about being left behind? •• Is it fair to be angry with Buster or Kate? •• What character traits might describe Lambert?

• • •

The Important When: 5,000 years ago
The Important Where: Mesopotamia

Kate could see she wasn't really alone. There were people working in the fields.

A man was walking toward Kate. He wore a helmet and a cape. He also wore a skirt made of cloth. A soldier? The man motioned to Kate. Not knowing what else to do, Kate fell in behind him. He was in a hurry.

The man handed Kate a silver ribbon as they walked. Soon they came to a big stone building.

The man took Kate to a room where twelve beautiful servants were gathered. Kate and the other women were given clay cups. Kate was confused. She looked at the cup in one hand and the silver ribbon in the other. •• Does the story tell you where Kate is? •• Do you think she is in a palace, a temple, or a tomb?

• • •

The Important When: The year 2300
The Important Where: Ms. X's classroom

Ms. X entered the classroom. Her students were visibly excited. Holograms of Kate and the twelve servants surrounded them.

The women wore flower headdresses. **They were made of gold and silver ribbons. The women wore beautiful long dresses, gold earrings, and strings of beads. Ms. X almost smiled at her class.** "I see you are paying attention." •• Why are the kids in class paying attention?

Then Ms. X said, "Kate was transported in error. She is in the Cradle of Civilization. Does anyone know where that is?" No one responded.

"Kate has arrived in the Mesopotamian city of Ur. She is being prepared to be buried with Queen Puabi." •• This sounds ominous. How so?

The kids said very little. They were confused. Buried? Someone asked, "Do you mean she will be buried alive?"

Ms. X looked grim. Then she said, "Quest will bring Kate back, but someone else must go."

Lambert sat with his arms crossed and said, "I am prepared."

Ms. X said, "Archaeologists have also found the bodies of male guards and servants who died with their rulers." •• What might happen to Lambert if he accepts the challenge?

Ms. X said, "If you undertake this challenge, the consequences may be unwelcome." •• What might the unwelcome consequences be?

Lambert nodded. He was confident. **He didn't ask about his fate. He didn't ask what would happen to him. Lambert did not like to be left out. He wanted to be transported.** He cared little about consequences. •• What is Lambert's goal?

Ms. X said, "First, you must pass this test. Where is Mesopotamia located?"

Lambert said, "In modern-day Iraq." •• Is Lambert correct?

Ms. X said, "Mesopotamia means . . ."

Lambert said, "The land between two rivers." •• Is Lambert correct?

Ms. X said, "Why are the rivers important?"

Lambert said, "Water, farming, crops, food." •• Is Lambert correct?

Ms. X raised one eyebrow. "Now tell me four reasons why this desolate place should be called the Cradle of Civilization."

Lambert said, "The Sumerians, the people who lived there, invented the wheel. They were the first to build irrigation systems to control water. They were the first to build cities. They were the first to have a written language." •• Did Lambert pass the test? •• Why?

With that, Kate was back at her desk. She had a silver ribbon in her hand. Ms. X nodded at Kate.

Kate was back, but Lambert was gone. •• What do you think Lambert's fate will be?

CHAPTER TWENTY-EIGHT

Ancient Mysteries

Informational

Mesopotamian artifact

S ome of our greatest mysteries are from the past. To unlock
those mysteries, scientists use the scientific method.

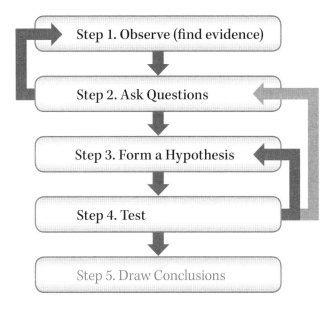

•• **Name the steps in the scientific method without looking.** •• Look at the arrow that goes from Step 4 to Step 2. The arrow shows that the method is recursive. What does that mean?

Sometimes people think they have solved a mystery, but new evidence can undo conclusions. New evidence can verify, challenge, or add to what we know. Knowledge evolves and grows over time. •• What happens to knowledge over time?

The Scientific Method and Archaeology

In 1922, Sir Woolley, a British archaeologist, began unearthing Mesopotamian burial sites in Iraq. Across twelve years, Woolley's team dug up 1,850 graves.

Woolley's stories about Mesopotamia were regularly reported in the newspapers. Woolley dug up 16 tombs in Ur — a city in the Mesopotamian empire of Babylonia. The tombs belonged to the kings and queens who lived thousands of years ago. (Kate's story took place in Ur. •• Was Kate's story of the silver ribbon fact or fiction?)

The Scientific Method and the Tombs in Mesopotamia

Step 1. Observe

In the tombs, Woolley found many things used by the kings and queens. He found artifacts — jewelry, statues, cosmetic shells, bowls, musical instruments, and even games that had been buried with the royalty.

Artifact from the tombs of Ur

Woolley also found the bodies of other people and animals. •• What did Woolley find in the tombs?

Step 2. Ask Questions

Woolley asked, "Who were the men and women in the tombs? Why were they buried with the kings and queens? How did they die?"

Step 3. Form Hypotheses

Based on what was found in the tombs, Woolley thought that the men and women were servants, musicians, and soldiers. Woolley had found clay cups in the grave. He hypothesized that the people had killed themselves so they could serve their kings and queens in the afterlife. •• What's another hypothesis?

Step 4. Test

Woolley had no way to test his hypothesis.

Step 5. Draw Conclusions

For many years, Woolley's best guess (or hypothesis) held up.

New Evidence

Recently, two researchers at the University of Pennsylvania had CT scans done on a male and female taken from the tombs. **The CT scan revealed round holes in the backs of their skulls. The people had been killed, but how?** •• Science has evolved. What invention allowed the scientists to learn more about the people who were killed?

New Conclusions

Did the people buried in the tombs commit suicide, as Woolley suggested? **No. Scientists found that at least some of the people in the mass graves were killed. Someone had ordered their demise.** •• Look at the picture on the next page. What do you think this tool may have been used for?

Tool used in
Mesopotamia

Striking End

Other Observations

One of the 16 royal tombs belonged to Queen Puabi. Near the queen's chamber were a wooden chest and the remains of oxen. **There were thirteen beautifully dressed women. One of the women had a silver ribbon in her hand.** •• What Quest character came back with a silver ribbon in her hand?

• • •

Woolley ended his archaeological digs in 1934. Since then, no other digs have taken place in Ur. •• Why do you think the digs stopped?

The Demise of Ur

About 4,000 years ago, Ur was destroyed. How? Historians think that Mesopotamia became too big to support its people. As Mesopotamia became bigger, more food was needed and the farmland was overused. The land became poor, so crops failed. **Written records and letters support the hypothesis that people were going hungry.** This led to unrest. Fires were set in the city. Farmland was torched and waterways ruined. •• Use evidence in the text to explain how Ur was destroyed.

CHAPTER TWENTY-NINE

And Then There Was One More

Narrative Fiction

Previously in the Third Quest

Kate had been sent to Mesopotamia by mistake. She had narrowly escaped being killed and then buried with Queen Puabi.

Lambert had passed a quiz and disappeared from class. And where was the team? They had been given an opportunity to send one team member back to the year 2300, but no one wanted to leave the team. •• What traits had the travelers demonstrated?

• • •

The Important When: The year 2300
The Important Where: Ms. X's classroom

In the blink of an eye, Kate had been returned to Ms. X's classroom. **Kate's classmates were standing and clapping. Kate felt dazed.** •• Why do you think Kate felt dazed?

Someone asked, "Were you scared?"

Kate frowned and then said, "Some of the women were

crying. Soldiers would not let them leave. I didn't know what was happening. It was all very confusing."

One of the kids said bluntly, "You were going to be killed so you could be buried with the queen. You were on a death march."

Kate turned white. Ms. X was watching and listening to her students. •• Is the class paying attention? Why?

Then someone said, "Hey, what happened to Lambert?"

Ms. X thought to herself, "Lambert — another Hill Academy kid — privileged but also a hothead." •• What do you think "privileged" means?

Ms. X said out loud, "Lambert passed the test. He has what he wanted. He wanted to be a time traveler. I don't know what his fate will be." •• What do we know about Lambert so far?

The kids were quiet. Then someone said, "What about the others?"

Ms. X said flatly, "I don't know what has happened to the team." •• Why do Ms. X's words sound ominous?

Ms. X left, and another note appeared on the wall.

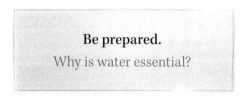

Be prepared.
Why is water essential?

This time, at least half the class was paying attention. Several of the kids began searching the school's database for answers. •• Why do you think more of the kids are paying attention? What is your hypothesis?

The Important When: 5,000 years ago
The Important Where: The City of Ur in Mesopotamia

In the blink of an eye, the team found themselves at a feast. Hundreds of people were milling around. There were plates of food. The team had been rewarded and sent forward in time to Mesopotamia. •• How has the team been rewarded?

Zack and Shack wore soldiers' outfits. Tuppins appeared to be a scribe. Anna and Ling looked like servants. They wore brown dresses. Mindy wore a beautiful long gown. She wore necklaces, earrings, bracelets, and rings of gold and precious-looking gems.

Mindy frowned, "I don't like this." •• Why is she unsettled?

Ling whispered to her. "It's just another test. Don't worry. We are in this together." •• Do you think Ling helped Mindy feel better? How would you describe Ling?

Mindy nodded her thanks. Then she noticed a loud commotion across the big hall. •• What do you think a "commotion" is?

People were shouting and pushing someone around. Mindy's mouth fell open. It was Lambert.

Lambert was an angry kid. He was a big bully, and Mindy did not like him. Shack and Zack were walking across the room. Shack grabbed Lambert and pulled him away from the scuffle. Then the boys escorted Lambert across the room. •• What do you think "escorted" means? •• Imagine Shack and Zack escorting Lambert across a big banquet room.

Anna looked at Lambert and said, "You are very lucky."

Mindy stared at Lambert and said, "Do not be a problem."

Lambert glared at Mindy. He wasn't happy. •• Glare at the person next to you. •• Why do you think Lambert is unhappy?

Before Lambert could say anything, Anna looked down. There was another folder under Tuppins' foot. Leaving Lambert sitting alone, the team huddled together to read another memo.

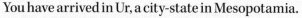

To: The Travelers
From: Quest Central
Date: The year 2300
Subject: An Unexpected Event

You have arrived in Ur, a city-state in Mesopotamia. Some people are wealthy and others are very poor. Soldiers may be sent into bloody battle, and servants may be sacrificed. You are in the court of Queen Puabi. Her death is impending. •• Describe Ur.

Make Lambert a team member. Welcome him and you will move forward. He will need to learn the rules.
  1. **Follow directions.**
  2. **Stick together.**
  3. **Do your part.**
  4. **Be respectful.**
  5. **Stay cool and calm.**

Good luck.

Anna said, "Maybe that's what he needs — some rules."

Shack said, "Memo's clear. We have no option." Then Shack said, "Hey, Lambert, if you want to be in, you are in."

Lambert was still seething. He did not smile. •• What do you think "seething" means?

Ling looked at Lambert. She waited. Then she gave Lambert a tray filled with food. •• Is Ling an asset? What makes you think so?

Tuppins did not say a word, but he was unsettled by Lambert. •• Why do you think Lambert made Tuppins feel unsettled?

CHAPTER THIRTY

Water!

Informational

Planet Earth

Imagine a colored photo of Earth from space. •• What do you see?

From space a planet slowly turns, revealing a surface covered mostly with water. Blue reflects the oceans. White swirling clouds reflect water caught temporarily in the planet's atmosphere. **This is the planet Earth. The planet is mostly water. We use that water every day, but we rarely think about it. How essential is water?** Ask yourself questions as you read. Intrigue and curiosity will follow.

Topic 1. An Essential

Water is in the cells of every living thing. In fact, without water, cells die. When cells die, life ends. **That means without water, any plant or animal will die. People can live about 30 days without food, but they can only live five to seven days without water.** •• What evidence in the text tells you that water is essential?

Conclusion: Every living thing needs water to live.

Topic 2. Water in Ancient Civilizations

For thousands of years, humans were nomads. Tribes moved on when water was hard to find. Then four great ancient civilizations appeared. **Each of these civilizations developed near rivers.** People learned to plant crops. **They also learned to control water so their crops survived.** As cities developed, more and more people depended on the crops. •• What did the four great civilizations have in common?

Conclusion: Civilizations depend on water.

Topic 3. Water Today

People use Earth's water every day. •• What do you use water for?

Did you know each person uses about:
- 25 gallons for a five-minute shower?
- 4 gallons of water every time a toilet is flushed?

In fact, we all use about 80 to 100 gallons of water every day.

Important Facts About Earth's Water

Living things need fresh water to survive, but there is very little fresh water on Earth.
- 97% of Earth's surface water is in the oceans
- 3% of Earth's water is fresh water
- Only 1% of Earth's water can be used for drinking

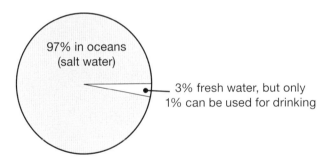

Conclusion: Fresh water is Earth's most important natural resource. •• Use evidence from the text to tell what you know about Earth's fresh water. •• What questions do you think scientists are asking about fresh water today?

CHAPTER THIRTY-ONE

Respect

Narrative Fiction

Previously in the Third Quest

The Quest memo had said, "Make Lambert a team member. Welcome him and you will move forward. He will need to learn the rules."

By their words and actions, Mindy, Zack, Shack, Anna, and Ling had told Lambert he was in — if he wanted. Tuppins stood by silent and unnoticed. Lambert had been too mad to respond. Things moved quickly. They were transported from harm's way. The ominous threat of death and separation in Mesopotamia had been removed. In the wink of an eye, the team traveled forward in time.

● ● ●

The Important When: 3,300 years ago
The Important Where: Ancient Egypt

Zack smiled. He was beginning to get used to the travels. He could see the Great Sphinx looming in the distance.

Zack looked at Tuppins and said, "Okay, kid. It looks

like we are in Egypt. Now what?"

Tuppins grinned. "It would indeed seem that we are in ancient Egypt — Giza, to be exact." Then with barely a breath he continued, "The pyramids are a feat of engineering and construction. They are the largest stone buildings on Earth, and they've been standing for 4,500 years.

"There are 2.3 million blocks of stone in the Great Pyramid alone. Each stone is 4,000 pounds, perhaps more." Squinting into the sun, Tuppins said, "The Great Pyramid is one of the Seven Wonders of the World. It is perfect. During the time it was built, they didn't even have wheels." •• What tells you the building of the Great Pyramid was impressive?

Lambert rolled his eyes. Then he got in Tuppins' face and sneered at him. Shack said, "Hey!" Zack stepped in between Lambert and Tuppins.

Lambert said, "Hey back at you! My computer, Buster, could do that. That kid is just a mindless computer." •• What does Lambert mean by "mindless computer"?

Zack and Shack both pushed Lambert away from Tuppins. Lambert's face turned red. He started to say something, but Anna stepped up and said, "Stop. Do not say another word. Breathe! You have to be a team member." •• What in the text tells that Lambert is angry? •• Why do you think Lambert was mean to Tuppins?

Then Anna said, "Lambert, you have no choice in this. We have to follow directions. **We have to stick together, do our parts, be respectful, and stay cool."**

Lambert started to say something, but Anna put her hand up. "Lambert, stop. We have to depend on you. You have to treat us all with respect." Anna could see that Lambert was still angry, but he had stopped. He had listened. Anna nodded at Lambert and said, "Thanks. We need your **help."** •• Do you think Anna is an asset? How did she help Lambert?

To: The Travelers Seven
Subject: An Asset

You have arrived in ancient Egypt — one of the four great river civilizations. **Human sacrifices happen here, but that will not be your fate.** Tuppins has earned the right to choose one topic he wishes to explore.

The Quest gives you a moment to rest and relax. Gain knowledge. It will serve you well.

Zack was impressed. Lambert was listening. •• Is Zack still aloof? Do you think he's a robot or an android?

Tuppins was silent. He stood aside, looking at his feet. Shack said, "Hey, Tuppins. You are good. The Egypt facts are cool."

Shack slapped Tuppins on the back. "You are an asset. You are a star. You are the king! So, what are we going to do here?"

Tuppins said, "Mummies." The kids nodded — even Lambert.

Mindy looked at Lambert and thought, "Maybe there's hope."

Ling was happy. She relaxed a little. •• How is Tuppins an asset? •• How did Shack show that he is an asset in this chapter?

• • •

The Important When: The year 2300
The Important Where: Ms. X's classroom

Ms. X listened to Lambert and Anna closely. She wondered if her class could tell what was happening. Anna had stepped up. And Lambert — well, that was interesting! Ms. X wondered whether he would learn to be a true team member. •• What does Lambert need to learn to be a team member?

CHAPTER THIRTY-TWO

Mummies It Is

Narrative Fiction

Previously in the Third Quest

The Important When: 3,300 Years Ago
The Important Where: Ancient Egypt

In the last memo, Tuppins had been rewarded by Quest Central for an unnamed accomplishment. He had earned the right to select one topic from ancient Egyptian history that he wished to experience. **Tuppins had chosen mummies.**

Tuppins did not understand people. He was not bothered by Lambert. But he had been upset by lost opportunities. Tuppins hadn't seen a dinosaur or a woolly mammoth. He had met a human from 40,000 years ago, but barely. Then the team had been transported from Mesopotamia before he had experienced being a scribe. Tuppins had felt unsettled, but now he was excited. •• Why had Tuppins felt unsettled?

• • •

Then, in the blink of an eye, the pyramid was gone. The six travelers stood inside a room. They were ghostlike and invisible. •• What does "in the blink of an eye" mean? •• Describe the team.

Shack went and stood in the middle of the room. He said, "Hello." No one in the room noticed him.

Ling whispered, "No one can see us or hear us, but where is Lambert?"

Shack said, "That dude didn't pass the test." •• What do you think happened to Lambert?

Ling said, "Look!" Lambert was helping three men carry in a body. Suddenly a terrible smell permeated the room.

Mindy covered her nose with both hands and said, "What is that?" •• What permeated the air?

Tuppins stepped forward and peered at the body. "It would appear that you are smelling rotting flesh. Look, the body has an open wound, and maggots are eating at the flesh." Ling stepped forward and took a close look. The others took a step back. •• What tells you that Ling has an inquiring mind? •• Describe the body.

Lambert helped the men carefully position the body on a bench. Lambert looked a little sick, but he didn't say a word. •• What questions do you have about Lambert?

Tuppins said, "Lambert appears to be part of the embalming team. It looks and smells like the body hasn't been cleaned yet. After they clean the body, they will start removing the body's organs."

Anna said, "Why?"

Tuppins said, "They are preparing the body for the afterlife. It is part of the process. They are making a mummy. They will leave the heart. The ancient Egyptians believed the heart was needed in the afterlife. **It was thought to be the center of thought and emotion. However, they removed the brain, stomach, intestines, and liver."** •• What do you think Ling is thinking?

Tuppins was watching the process intently, but said, **"It is quite apparent that the ancient Egyptians didn't fully understand how the body works.** Nonetheless, their mummification practices were quite advanced."

The men carefully cleaned the body. Then a man lifted a hooked tool and pushed it with great force up the body's nose. Lambert looked startled. •• Why is Lambert startled?

Shack said, "Hey! Did you see that?"

Next, the men took turns pushing the tool around and pulling something out of the nose. It was Lambert's turn. He was very serious. **The team watched. Zack whispered, "Lambert is stepping up."**

Tuppins and Ling leaned in to watch. The others kept their distance, but felt compelled to watch. •• What in the text tells you Tuppins and Ling are interested?

Tuppins said, "Maybe the body belongs to King Tut. Scientists think he may have died from a wound that became infected."

The men turned the body on its side. One of the men cut a large slit down its side. Lambert helped steady the body.

Shack shook his head. **"Man, look at Lambert. He's still standing. I got to give him respect for that." The others nodded.**

The work Lambert was doing was gruesome, but he had

stayed with it. •• What is Lambert learning? •• What in the text makes you think that? •• It says "the work Lambert was doing was gruesome." What does that mean?

• • •

The Important When: The year 2300
The Important Where: Quest Central

Ms. X was standing and six other scientists were sitting around a table. They were all intently watching the team. Ms. X said, "Thank you for coming. We are here to determine what happens next. The team has evolved in rather nice ways." •• How has the team evolved?

A scientist spoke. "Dr. X, I am confused about Lambert. He is an interesting subject, but I did not see him in the research proposal."

Dr. X said, "Lambert was an accident." •• Who is Dr. X? •• What questions do you have for Dr. X?

CHAPTER THIRTY-THREE

Inheriting From the Past
Informational

Mysteries and Inquiring Minds

From hunter-gatherers to farmers, from village dwellers to city builders, across time people have invented new ways to do things.

Knowledge Builds on Knowledge

People have inquiring minds. They pursue mysteries and solve problems. They invent new ways of doing things and pass knowledge to the next generation. Knowledge builds on knowledge. •• What do you think "knowledge builds on knowledge" means?

Six to seven thousand years ago, the people of Mesopotamia invented many things we still use today. •• What did we inherit from the people of Mesopotamia?

Archaeology

Today, archaeologists dig to uncover our past. They risk their lives in dark tunnels looking for things left by the dead — mummies and artifacts from the past. They work carefully to remove, transport, and preserve what they find. They keep records and then study the objects. Archaeologists use the scientific method to solve mysteries and understand the past. •• What are the steps in the scientific method?

Like other scientists, archaeologists persevere in search of answers. •• Why do you think archaeologists work so patiently to uncover the past?

I LOVE ARCHAEOLOGY.
It is my passion, my reason for living.
We bring the past to life.
Zahi Hawass, Archaeologist

Needed!
Inquiring minds

Ancient Egyptian Pyramids

Observations

The early Egyptians built elaborate tombs. The Great Pyramid of Giza is the tomb of a pharaoh — a ruler in Egypt. The pyramid rises 482 feet into the sky — about the same as a 30-story building. It was built from stone blocks. Just one stone block was 4,000–5,000 pounds, weighing as much as two cars. Over two million of these massive stone blocks were used to build the Great Pyramid.

The Great Pyramid was built about 4,500 years ago. There were no carts. Wheels were not in use yet. They only had simple tools.

Questions

How did the Egyptians move the massive stones to build the Great Pyramid? How did the Egyptians cut and move the stone blocks into place?

Hypotheses

Many hypotheses have been proposed over the years. Some people have asked if the pyramid was constructed by aliens. Or was the pyramid carved from a massive stone hill?

Scientists think thousands of workers were hired to build the Great Pyramid. It would have taken thousands of workers over 20 years to build the massive pyramid. Scientists think the stones were dragged across the sands with sleds and then moved into place using ramps. •• Let's stop and picture the Egyptian workers moving the huge stones across the sand.

The Evidence

1. A painting from 4,000 years ago shows 173 men hauling a huge statue with ropes and a sled. A person can be seen on the front of the sled pouring water over the sand.

Scientists at the University of Amsterdam constructed sleds. They could pull heavy objects across the sand if the correct amount of water was added to the sand.

2. Once the stones were at the construction site, the workers would have dragged the stones up ramps. The ramps would have been built of mud, brick, and plaster. One ramp still exists.

On digs, archaeologist Donald Redford has helped a

team of 20 workers pull up a 5,000-pound stone using only ropes. He knows firsthand that it can be done.

3. Archaeologists Hawass and Lehner found the remains of bakeries and other rooms that may have been used to prepare food for the workers. **These scientists think the workers were treated well.**

•• Look back in the text. What evidence is there that the huge stones were moved by men using ropes, sleds, and wet sand?

Drawing Conclusions: The Evidence Builds

People today would not attempt to build a massive pyramid with only sleds, ropes, and water. Many questions remain, but the riddle is mostly solved. **The Great Pyramid, one of the Seven Wonders of the World, appears to have been built by thousands of people who had to plan, work together, and persevere.** •• Why wouldn't people today try to build a pyramid with only sleds, ropes, and water?

Coming Up: The Wonders of Making Mummies

CHAPTER THIRTY-FOUR

The Mummy's Curse
Informational

The people of ancient Egypt believed that death was a doorway to eternal life. They hoped to live forever in a perfect world.

Mummies

The ancient Egyptians believed they would need their bodies in the afterlife. Dead bodies decay, so the Egyptians preserved them for the afterlife. The preserved bodies are called mummies. •• Why did the ancient Egyptians make mummies?

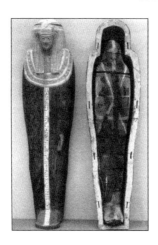

Sarcophagus and mummy inside

When were Egyptian mummies made? Today, scientists study Egyptian mummies. Some of the mummies are as old as 5,500 years; others are only 2,500 years old. The Egyptians made mummies for about 3,000 years, and then they stopped. •• When were mummies made? •• What questions do you have about mummies?

A Greek traveler wrote eyewitness accounts of life in Egypt 2,500 years ago. Modern science has verified his reports of mummy making. The process took seventy days.

Step 1: Getting Ready. The body was washed. Then it was taken to a special house to get ready for burial.

Step 2: Organs Removed. Organs decay quickly, so they were removed. A bronze hook was inserted into one of the body's nostrils and pushed hard. The brain was broken down and then drained through the nose. The brain was thought to be useless, so it was thrown away.

A cut was made on the side of the body. Then the organs were lifted out by hand and taken away to be mummified. The heart was left in place because it was thought to be the center of thinking and reason. •• Which organ did the Egyptians think controlled thought?

Step 3: Cleaned, Packed, and Preserved. The body was cleaned out with water and wine. Then the body was packed with rags, straw, and bags of natron — a natural preservative with a high salt content. Natron soaks up moisture and was used by fishermen to preserve fish.

Step 4: Set Out to Dry Out. Next, the body was covered with 500 pounds of natron. **The body was left to dry for 40 days. This process made the body black and withered.** •• How was the body kept from rotting?

Step 5: Cleaned, Unpacked, and Perfumed. After the body was washed again, the bags of preservative were removed. Then the body was refilled with cloth, sawdust, and mud. The skin was carefully rubbed with oils and perfumes.

Step 6: Hardened. The body was covered with hot pitch from pine trees. This resin would harden as it cooled. •• What does "resin" mean as used in the last sentence?

Step 7: Eyes and Hair Added. **False eyes and a wig were added to the body.**

Step 8: Wrapped. The body was wrapped in 20 layers of cloth strips.

Step 9: Stiffened. More resin was poured over the mummy so it would harden. **The mummies were so stiff they could stand.** •• What are some interesting facts about mummy making?

Step 10: Ready. The body and mummified organs were returned to the family for burial. **The organs were placed with the body. The body was placed in a coffin — a house for the person's life force.**

Step 11: Buried. The journey to the afterlife began on the day of the burial. **The Egyptians thought the dead could eat, drink, hear, see, and smell in the afterlife.**

The royals and the wealthy were buried with food, furniture, statues, artwork, and jewelry. Members of the royal staff were buried with their kings and queens. **They were human sacrifices.** •• How are these customs the same as or different from today's customs?

Grave Robbers

Since the earliest days of Egypt, robbers have sneaked into the tombs and taken from the dead — even before the tombs were sealed. Who were the culprits? Archaeologists think that gravediggers, tomb builders, and even priests raided the tombs. •• Why would people rob from the graves?

The Egyptians tried to protect their gravesites. The kings and queens went to great lengths to hide them. The entrances to the pyramids were blocked so no one could find them. Inside the pyramids, there were hidden passages.

Mummies and their treasures were hidden in mazes built under the pyramids. Warnings were written to keep intruders away. **The warnings were curses from the dead.**

Beware. Do no evil to the tomb.
The spirits will haunt anyone who disturbs the resting place of ancient Egyptians.

•• Do you think grave robbers disrupted the ancient Egyptians' journey to the afterlife? •• Do you think grave robbers were haunted by the dead?

The Quest Evolves
Narrative Fiction

Previously in the Third Quest

Lambert was working with an embalming team. The travelers were impressed with his professionalism and teamwork.

The Important When: The year 2300
The Important Where: Quest Central
The Important Who: A team of scientists

•• What do you think the scientists are studying?

Dr. X (aka Ms. X) and six other scientists were sitting around a table. Dr. X said, "We need to decide whether to bring the travelers home." •• Who is Dr. X? What do you think is her true identity?

Dr. X said, "Each of the travelers has stepped up, even Lambert. No one expected the team from 2100 to be exceptional. However, members of Quest 2100 became a U.S. president, a Nobel Peace Prize winner, a Supreme Court justice, an inventor, and an Olympic track star.

Dr. X said, "The fate of this team is also looking promising. They have demonstrated grit and teamwork." •• What do you think "grit" means?

"This is our hypothesis: If, under difficult circumstances, teens develop perseverance, integrity, teamwork, and professionalism, they will become great leaders."

Dr. X said, "The team needs more time to mature. They need to use their heads. There are more challenges ahead for them."

After a moment of reflection, Dr. Kumar said, "Let's continue. Just be sure to bring everyone home."

Dr. X thought, "This is good." However, the longer the team traveled, the harder it would be to bring them back. The team of 2200 had simply vanished.

Dr. X slipped into a private observation pod. Lambert was still working with a team of embalmers. Dr. X could not allow this team to vanish — not even Lambert. It was a heavy responsibility.

The Quest had begun as a game in 2100. Then, in 2200, the game had been repeated, but the team had been lost. Now, Quest Central was repeating the game again and studying how the team was developing. Parent permission had been granted before the Quest began. •• What was the Quest in 2100? •• Why do you think parents gave their permission for the 2300 team to participate?

• • •

The Important When: **3,300 years ago** (in the time of King Tutankhamun [toot an KAH men] aka King Tut)

The Important Where: The embalmers' tent

The Important Who: Lambert and the team of six

The travelers wandered around the embalmers' tent unseen and unheard by the Egyptians in the room. Mindy was standing near Lambert. She was saying, "Don't, Lambert."

Anna looked up to see what was happening. Lambert had a gold object in his hand. Anna said, "Lambert, you've done so well. This isn't the time to take a souvenir!"

Lambert didn't hear a word, but he placed the charm in the cloth wrappings and stepped back.

Shack gave a thumbs-up. With that, Lambert found himself standing with the team of six, invisible to the embalmers. Shack whacked Lambert on the back. Zack said, "Impressive." •• What character traits had Lambert shown?

Ling nodded, "We are very proud of you."

Lambert wasn't sure what to say. Tuppins filled the silence. "About 3,351 years ago, King Tut took the throne and ruled all of Egypt. He was only ten and ruled for eight or nine years. Tut inherited the throne when the Egyptians had conquered their enemies and become powerful traders. Egypt was rich and powerful under Tut.

"After his death, the Egyptians believed that King Tut would be transformed into a god. It seems you were preparing the young king to be a god. Your task was quite important."

Lambert was listening intently to every word. •• How has Lambert's character evolved? •• Would you want him to be on your team? Why or why not?

CHAPTER THIRTY-SIX

Study Up
Narrative Fiction

Previously in the Third Quest

Kate had been transported to Mesopotamia and sent on a death march. Lambert had passed a quiz and taken her place.

Lambert had been given a difficult task. Do you remember what that was? •• How did Lambert meet the Quest requirements when on the embalming team?

• • •

Ms. X placed her foot on a small round device and found herself back at the decrepit school. Her students were staring intently at the holograms. One of the kids said, "Did you see that? The team is congratulating Lambert." •• Why is the team congratulating Lambert?

Ms. X cleared her throat and made the images disappear. Then she put on the meanest old face she could muster. She said sternly, "Class, be seated.

"You will need to pass a test the next time we meet. I've prepared a study guide for you. Practice answering the

questions out loud with a partner. Do not delay. Remember what happened to Kate."

Kate looked up. She didn't understand what she had to do with a test, but the other kids seemed to be listening. The kids were partnering up.

Ms. X said, "You will study shortly. Take turns quizzing one another."

Ms. X displayed instructions:

1. Have your partner cover the answers. Ask your partner a question. Give your partner time to think.
2. Check the answer and help as needed.
3. Keep asking the question until the answer is easy.

Then, switch roles for the next question. Keep practicing any hard questions. Practice should be recursive. •• What does "recursive" mean as used in the sentence?

Ms. X said, "You should be able to answer each question with confidence." Then, as if it were a race, Ms. X said, "Ready, begin."

Kate smiled at Ms. X. Then she got to work with her partner. •• Why did Kate smile at Ms. X? •• I'll be your partner. Cover the answers on the next page, and I will quiz you.

Study Guide for Levels 4 and 5

Question	Answer
1. What are three important reasons that Mesopotamia is considered the Cradle of Civilization?	They were the first to develop: • big farms and irrigation • big cities • the wheel • a writing system • a number system
2. Why were early great civilizations located near rivers?	The river provided water for farming.
3. Describe what the Egyptians believed about the afterlife.	They believed the afterlife was forever, happy, and perfect.
4. How did wealthy Egyptians prepare for the afterlife?	Wealthy people were made into mummies. They were buried in fine tombs with many things and people to serve them.
5. Are the chapters about the Third Quest team fact or fiction?	The story about the team and travel to the past is made up. There are facts in the story, but the story is fiction.
6. What did wealthy Egyptians have that other people did not?	Look back in the text for evidence to support your answer.

•• What should you do to get ready for the Level 5 quiz?

Ms. X watched as her students started working. She was worried about those who didn't study. She was worried about those who were habitually late — late for class, late getting their work in, late! School would be hard. They would not get good jobs. •• Who is Ms. X worried about?

She hovered over them. If someone was goofing off, she said, "Perhaps you will get a silver ribbon." •• That's a bit ominous. Why do you think Ms. X mentions the silver ribbon?

Ms. X slowly circulated through the class. She said nothing, but the kids could almost hear her say:

Work hard.

Be prepared.

Practice!

•• Explain how Ms. X is getting into the students' heads.

•• Explain how the class is getting into Ms. X's head.

CHAPTER THIRTY-SEVEN

A Belief in Many Gods

Informational

Introduction

Ancient Egypt was a land with little rain. The land was a dry and barren desert. A small strip of land along the Nile River provided Egypt's people with food.

Every year the Nile flooded, leaving behind rich farmland. The people depended on the yearly floods. Without flooding, the crops were poor and the people went hungry. •• Were the yearly floods essential? Why?

The Role of the Gods

The ancient Egyptians believed the gods created life and controlled their fate. Stories of the gods explained why things happened. The people believed the gods were responsible for all that was good and all that was bad.

The ancient Egyptians believed the yearly floods were a gift from the gods. If the floods did not come, the people believed the gods were angry. **Pleasing the gods was essential.** •• Why were the gods so important to the Egyptian people?

Many Gods and Goddesses

In Egypt, the people believed in many gods and goddesses. Ra, the sun god, was the most important. **He created the other gods and was the most powerful of the gods. Ra created Earth, water, air, land, and all living things.** •• What in the text explains why Ra was the most important god?

Under Ra, there were hundreds of gods and goddesses. These gods were central to Egyptian lives. The Egyptians believed that they had to keep the gods happy in their earthly homes. Temples were built to the gods, and gifts or offerings were taken to them. •• What did the people do to keep the gods happy?

Bastet, the Goddess of Cats

Bastet, the goddess of cats, was a daughter of Ra. **She was a goddess of protection.** Her religious center was the city of Bubastis.

Like many gods, Bastet evolved over time. At first, she was a warrior and shown as a lion. **Over time, she was worshipped as a mother and often portrayed in statues and paintings as a cat with kittens.**

Every year, thousands of visitors traveled by ship to Bastet's festival. As they traveled the Nile, there was music, song, and dance. The people drank wine and made great sacrifices to the goddess. •• If you were an Egyptian, would you have worshipped the gods? Why or why not? •• What gifts do you think people took to Bastet?

Bastet, goddess of cats

Headlines from History

Knowledge of our past continues to grow as new evidence is found. People continue to find previously unknown places that the ancient Egyptians built. A few headlines from the study of ancient Egyptians follow.

Cat Mummies by the Thousands

1888, Istabl Antar, Egypt (about 250 years ago)

Digging in the sand, a farmer uncovered a mass grave. The grave held the mummies of ancient cats — hundreds of thousands of cats. Some of the mummies were painted with gold. •• Why do you think the cats were mummified and buried in just one place?

The best cat mummies were sold to tourists. **Other cat mummies were sold and shipped by the thousands to England. In England, the mummies were ground up and used on farms for fertilizer.** •• What in the text makes you think the English did not think the mummies were sacred?

More than 300,000 cat mummies have been found buried under Bastet's temple.

Dog Mummies by the Millions

2015, Cairo, Egypt •• How many years ago was 2015?

Recently, an estimated 8 million dog mummies were found in underground tombs. The mummies were located under a temple dedicated to the god Anubis — god of the afterlife.

Anubis, god of
the afterlife

Archaeologist Salima Ikram writes that the Egyptians made animal mummies as offerings to the gods. **She says, "Instead of a candle, they would offer a mummy."**

The archaeologist has hypothesized that the Egyptians even raised puppies to be killed as offerings to the god. As horrible as this seems in modern times, the Egyptians believed the dogs were going to a better afterlife. •• What are some of the ways the ancient Egyptians differ from people today?

CHAPTER THIRTY-EIGHT

The Parents

Narrative Fiction

Previously in the Third Quest

As part of an embalming team, Lambert had demonstrated integrity, perseverance, teamwork, and professionalism. The travelers had been impressed.

Back in the classroom, Ms. X had given her students a study guide and told them to work in partners. To anyone goofing off, Ms. X warned, "Perhaps you will get a silver ribbon!" •• What does the silver ribbon mean? •• Why is the silver ribbon an ominous sign?

• • •

The Important When: The year 2300
The Important Where: Quest Central, parents' meeting

Mindy's parents had demanded a meeting with Quest. They were upset. Mr. Herzig said forcefully, "Mindy needs to come home. That's it. There's nothing to discuss. We want her home."

Ms. X thought, "He is arrogant." But she said, "As you wish." •• Why does Ms. X think Mr. Herzig is arrogant?

In the blink of an eye, Mindy was standing next to her parents. Startled, Mr. and Mrs. Herzig jumped up and hugged her. There was a commotion. Everyone wanted to ask Mindy questions. •• What do you think the parents asked?

Mindy looked around and asked, "Where are the others?"

Ms. X said, "They are still in the past."

A look of alarm crossed Mindy's face. "I don't understand."

Mr. Herzig said, "I decided to bring you back. It was too dangerous."

Mindy said, "But I voted to stay. I can't abandon the others."

Mr. Herzig said, "Enough. Going back is not an option."

Mindy hesitated and then said, "I voted to stay."

Mr. Herzig repeated, "No. What's next? A famine? A flood? A war?"

Mindy looked to Ms. X for help, but Ms. X shook her head and said, "Quest requires parent permission."

Mindy's eyes filled with tears. •• Why is Mindy upset?

Ms. X looked at the other parents. "You each have the power to change the fate of your child."

Shack's mother said, "This is Shack's decision. He voted to stay." •• How is Shack's mother different from Mindy's father? •• Do they both care about their children?

Lambert's parents were out of the country. Buster, Lambert's computer guardian, was there via Internet. Buster said, "Please excuse my lack of human form. Lambert will stay. The Quest is helping Lambert learn integrity." •• Where are Lambert's parents? •• Do you think Buster should decide Lambert's fate?

Next, Mr. and Mrs. Tuppins spoke. Mr. Tuppins said, "Tup loves the past. Tup is . . . well, different, but he is making friends. We want him to stay."

Just then, the holograms of Anna and Ling appeared. Anna was shouting, "Where is Mindy?"

• • •

The Important When: About 3,300 years ago
The Important Where: Ancient Egypt

A huge frog was sitting on a blue folder. Anna lifted the frog off the folder and began reading.

> To: The Travelers
> From: Quest Central
> Date: The year 2300
> Subject: The Parents
>
> Mindy has been sent back to 2300. Shack and Tuppins will stay.
>
> Anna and Ling, your parents request an answer. Will you stay?

Ling said, "Quest is watching us."
Anna said, "It doesn't matter. I'm staying."
Ling said, "I'm staying, too, but I will miss Mindy."
Anna looked at Lambert. "You need to be part of the team."

Lambert didn't know what to say. **As was his habit, he rolled his eyes. Zack looked at Lambert and said, "You proved yourself. Now, you have a chance to be part of the team. If I were you, I'd check your attitude somewhere else."**
•• What do you think "check your attitude somewhere else" means?

Shack was smiling. The *Beelzebufo* was sitting on his shoulder. He had another memo in his very big mouth. Shack gave the memo to Zack.

To: Zack
From: Kayla and James Jefferson
Date: The year 2300
Subject: Message for Zack

You must finish the Quest. You will be free of our damaged reputation. You can prove yourself and become an important man.

We love you. We are sorry to have been a burden.

Zack looked at the others and simply said, "I'm in."
•• Zack is a mysterious character. At first, Mindy thought he might be an android because he was so aloof. Where do you think Zack's parents are? •• Do you think Zack is an android?

Tuppins didn't like change. With Mindy gone and Lambert joining the team, Tuppins felt unsettled again.

From the year 2300, Mindy was watching. She thought, "I'm with you all, and I will get back."

CHAPTER THIRTY-NINE

Computer Malfunction

Narrative Fiction

Previously in the Third Quest

Lambert and the team had been reunited in Egypt, but Mindy had been sent back to the year 2300. Mindy's parents had demanded that she be returned. The others had been allowed to stay, but each for a different reason.

• • •

The Important When: The year 2300
The Important Where: Ms. X's classroom

Ms. X handed out the test. Then she said, "You have been training for this test. You should do well. Doing poorly may have unintended consequences." Then Ms. X left the room. On display were the words:

> **Check your answers!**

The kids looked around. Kate's expression was serious. She was thinking, "Do your best. Read each question carefully. Check your answers."

When the last student finished, the holograms appeared, but then there was a loud crunching sound. There was a commotion in the classroom. Melvin said, "That sound. We've heard that sound before." Then, just as the Quest logo had disintegrated, the holograms disintegrated. •• What do you think the sound and the disintegrating holograms foreshadow, or predict?

• • •

The Important Where: Egypt
The Important When: About 3,300 years ago

Lambert sat on a bench while the others huddled. He still didn't know how to be a team member. The others walked over to him. Anna said, "Lambert, you have a place on our team. We will help you."

Lambert looked up and started to say something, but there was a loud crunching sound. Lambert was suddenly gone. Poof — magic! The five remaining students looked at each other. Then the ominous sound repeated. •• Why is the sound ominous?

• • •

Anna and Ling looked around. They stood on a stone pathway. A giant stone wall stretched as far as they could see. Ling said, "China."

• • •

In another location, Lambert stood face to face with a clay soldier.

• • •

Tuppins, Zack, and Shack stood under a blue sky. Just beyond them, a city rose out of the desert. Zack turned to Tuppins and asked, "Where are we?" •• Are the kids together?

Tuppins got an unsettled feeling. Then he rubbed the top of his head and said, "I do not know." •• Why does Tuppins feel unsettled?

Shack said, "It looks like the girls aren't here."

Zack said, "Lambert isn't here either." •• What questions do you have about what's happening?

• • •

The Important When: The year 2300
The Important Where: Quest Central's Computer Lab

Dr. X and two other research scientists stood staring at three huge screens. Dr. X said, "What has happened?"

Dr. Popov said, "The transporter malfunctioned. There could be an error in the code. We did not get an error message, so perhaps it's a mistake in the program's logic. The program may perceive Lambert as an invader. We just don't know what happened yet."

Dr. X tried to hide her emotions, but she was shaken. The results could be tragic. •• What is Dr. X thinking?

The room was silent. Finally, Dr. X said, "So we have

many hypotheses, but no answers. Where are my students now?"

A young technician spoke up. "Ling and Anna are at the Great Wall of China. **We do not know the year yet, but it is ancient China.**"

Dr. X said, "And Lambert. I can see he is China, in the tomb of Emperor Qin (chin). Qin was buried in 210 BCE. **So Lambert could be in China anywhere from 2,500 years ago to now.**"

•• Where are Ling and Anna? •• Where is Lambert?

Dr. X asked, "**And where are Zack and Tuppins? I don't recognize where they are.**"

Another lab worker said, "The boys are in the Indus Valley, maybe about 5,000 years ago."

Dr. X said, "**That's why Tuppins doesn't know where he is.** The Indus Valley was one of the world's greatest early civilizations, but most of the world hasn't heard of it."

The scientists stood looking at the three huge screens. They all looked grim. No one said a word, but they were all thinking about Quest 2200. The malfunction was an ominous event. •• What do you think might happen to the Quest 2300 team?

CHAPTER FORTY

The Indus Valley

Informational

Introduction

The Mesopotamians and Egyptians built the first two of four great river civilizations. A third great civilization, the Indus Valley, developed around 2600 BCE, about 600 years after the first cities were built in Mesopotamia. •• Which civilization was built first — Mesopotamia or the Indus Valley?

The Indus Valley civilization was located in modern-day Pakistan and India. It included over 1,000 cities. Despite its size, it simply vanished. For thousands of years, no one knew that it even existed. •• What happened to the civilization?

River valleys were essential to the early great civilizations. Like Mesopotamia and Egypt, the Indus Valley civilization was built on a floodplain. •• Look at the map on the next page. Find the Indus Valley civilization. What river supported the Indus Valley civilization?

Discovery

In 1826, a British army deserter came across brick mounds in the desert. Later he wrote of his travels and wondered if the

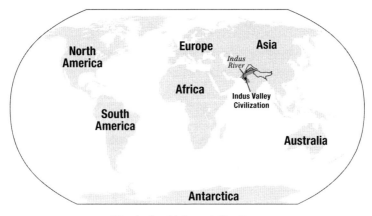

The Indus Valley civilization

brick mounds were the remains of an old castle.

Then in 1856, railway workers found more bricks. The workers used the bricks to form beds for their railway tracks. Among the bricks, seals were found. The artifacts and man-made bricks were a sign that the remains of an ancient civilization lay under the desert sand. •• Look at the picture. Read the caption. What observations can you make about the Indus Valley people?

Seal and stamp crafted in the Indus Valley

Finally, in the 1920s, archaeologists began excavating to see where the bricks and seals came from. Two forgotten cities, Harappa (huh-RAP-uh) and Mohenjo-daro (moh-HEN-joh DAHR-oh), slowly emerged from the desert.

Excavation of Indus Valley city

Accomplishments

Unlike the other ancient river civilizations, the people of the Indus Valley did not leave behind great temples, tombs, or mummies. Archaeologists think they did *not* have all-powerful rulers or gods who demanded that monuments be built for them.

What did the people of the Indus Valley accomplish? They had the most advanced water systems of all the early civilizations.

- The people built huge man-made lakes to store flood-water for their cities.
- **They used underground water for drinking. Many homes had a well for fresh water.**
- **They built tiled bathrooms in their homes.** The bathrooms had a toilet and an underground drainage system to carry away waste.

The people of Mesopotamia and Egypt did not have bathrooms. They did not have sewage systems to remove wastewater. It was over a thousand years before the Romans had baths, toilets, and sewage systems. •• Find evidence in the text that explains what made the Indus Valley water systems the most advanced of their time. •• Would you have rather lived in Mesopotamia, Egypt, or the Indus Valley? Explain why.

The people of the Indus Valley built cities that were carefully planned. The streets were paved and built in grids. City blocks were square. Clearly, the Harappans were well organized. •• Imagine a city laid out in grids. What would a map look like?

Scientists have found little evidence of weapons in the remains. The people of the Indus Valley did not engage in ongoing wars. Instead, the people farmed and built cities. They made crafts, and they traded with others, including the Mesopotamians. •• Use text evidence to explain why scientists think the Harappans were peaceful.

The Indus Valley people may have been the most advanced of the early civilizations, but also the most mysterious. The Harappans had a writing system. But unlike Sumerian cuneiform and Egyptian hieroglyphics, no one has been able to figure out how to read the Harappan writing. •• Why do we know so little about the Harappans?

The Biggest Mystery

In about 1900 BCE (3,900 years ago), the Indus Valley civilization disappeared. The people gradually left its cities. They abandoned their homes. Then, over thousands of years, the desert sands covered its remains. •• What questions do you have about the Indus Valley?

CHAPTER FORTY-ONE

Error Detection

Narrative Fiction

A transporter malfunction had created a controlled panic in the computer lab at Quest Central. The team had been sent to different places and perhaps different times. •• The malfunction was an ominous event. Why?

• • •

The Important Where: Quest Central
The Important When: The year 2300

Dr. X stood talking privately with Dr. Kumar, head of Quest Central. **Dr. X said, "We need to solve this problem quickly." Then she said, "We need Buster and Homer."**

Dr. Kumar looked surprised. "Lambert's guardian and the library computer?"

Dr. X said, "I did some research. Buster and Homer are XB-2200 and XH-2200. **They were in charge of programming Quest 2200.** They were two of the finest androids ever produced."

Dr. Kumar said, "I know the story, but they were taken

apart when Quest 2200 failed."

Dr. X said, "People were prejudiced against the droids and wanted them destroyed. **A team of scientists did not agree. They hid the robots by putting their hard drives in a couple of ordinary computers. The scientists believed Homer and Buster were unfairly blamed. They believed human error resulted in the transporter malfunction."** •• Why did the team of scientists hide Homer and Buster?

Dr. X asked, "May I bring Homer and Buster here to the lab?"

● ● ●

Moments later, Dr. Kumar watched as two white-haired men greeted one another. The androids, Buster and Homer, **had been reinstalled in their human forms. Dr. Kumar noticed how human-like they were.** No one would ever have guessed that they were androids.

Homer and Buster looked like humans. They sounded like humans. They had human traits. •• Use text evidence to explain what made the androids seem totally human.

About twenty scientists had gathered. The robots were famous. Homer took charge. He asked, "What is our priority?"

Buster said, "No one is missing, but the Quest 2300 travelers are in different places and different times."

Homer said, "So, *who* is the priority?"

Buster said, "Ling and Anna are in the greatest danger. My ward, Lambert, is safe until he runs out of food and water. He is with the terra-cotta army in China. He has a life-sized army of eight thousand men to play with." An image of life-sized clay soldiers and horses flashed across a huge screen at the front of the lab. •• Do you think Lambert is safe? Why or why not?

The screen showed Lambert getting up on a horse's back. A yellow baseball cap hung on the horse's ear. •• Why do you think the yellow baseball cap is in the story? •• How would you have felt alone in a tomb?

Homer zeroed in on the word "ward." "Buster, did you say Lambert is your ward?"

Buster said proudly, "Yes, I am responsible for Lambert until his parents come back."

Homer raised one eyebrow and said, "You? A guardian computer?" •• Use text evidence to explain how Homer and Buster are demonstrating human traits.

Dr. X interrupted, "Zack, Shack, and Tuppins are in the Indus Valley. They are safe. The people of the Indus Valley were peaceful."

Homer said, "We will start with Ling and Anna. We need to move everyone forward to one place. From there, they can continue to safety."

Dr. X said, "I'd like to bring Lambert home. I am proud of him. He has evolved, but he has old habits to grow out of. He is not ready for the responsibilities given to Quest leaders." •• Why does Dr. X think Lambert should come home?

Buster brought up the computer code. The program was massive. Thousands of lines of code began streaming across the screen — too fast for the human eye to read. Buster and Homer peered at the code. You could hear a pin drop.

Buster said, "Back up forty thousand lines."

In seconds, Homer said, "Stop. That's the China code, and there is an error." Homer quickly typed something and then said, "I can bring Lambert home in a keystroke."

Dr. X said, "If it won't slow things down, go ahead and bring Lambert back first." Homer touched another key.

The scientists looked at the screen and broke into applause. The robots had shown how advanced they were. Buster laughed and took a bow. Homer looked up and smiled. •• Why did the scientists applaud? •• What human traits are the androids showing?

CHAPTER FORTY-TWO

Ancient China

Informational

Introduction

China is a huge country on the continent of Asia. To the south and east, great rivers flow through fertile farmland. To the north and west are tall mountains, dry grasslands, and vast deserts. Find ancient China on the map.

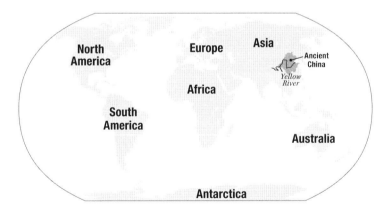

A Familiar Story

Seven thousand years ago, small tribes of hunter-gatherers traveled across China. By about six thousand years ago (4000 BCE), people had developed farming on the fertile

floodplains of the Yellow River. •• What do you think a "fertile floodplain" is? Look at the map again and find the Yellow River. •• Use text evidence and the map to describe China.

Like the people of Mesopotamia, Egypt, and the Indus Valley, these people learned to control water and grow food for their communities. **Their farms produced enough food to be stored from one season to the next. To the north, people continued their nomadic lives, sometimes invading the south.** •• How was the development of ancient China similar to that of Mesopotamia, Egypt, and the Indus Valley?

By 475 BCE, China had developed into seven king-doms — each with its own language, money system, and ruler. The seven kingdoms were often at war with one another.

The kingdom of Qin (chin) had a fierce army. **Soldiers were paid only after they had given their generals the cutoff heads of enemy warriors.** •• What do you think the ruler of the kingdom of Qin was like?

The First Emperor

In 247 BCE, a thirteen-year-old boy inherited the Qin throne. The boy-emperor had three goals. **1) He wanted to conquer the six other kingdoms. 2) He wanted to be the most powerful ruler in all of China. 3) He wanted to build the greatest tomb ever.** •• What were the goals of the new Qin ruler?

By 221 BCE, Qin's army had defeated the other kingdoms and established the first Chinese empire. At 38 years of age, Qin named himself Qin Shi Huang (chin shir hwong) — first emperor, God in Heaven, and All-Mighty Universe. Qin was both brilliant and vicious. •• Was Qin arrogant? How so?

Qin's Accomplishments

As the first emperor of China, Qin accomplished many things. He made everyone use one system of money and measurement. He ordered the use of a single written language, the oldest written language still in use today. He linked his vast kingdom with canals and roads. He also began the building of the Great Wall of China to defend the borders from the nomadic people of the north. •• What did Qin accomplish?

The Great Wall of China

Qin's Cruelty

The first emperor was also a cruel tyrant. He was hated by those he ruled. Qin believed that people were evil. He thought well-educated people were hard to control. He had all books burned, except those on medicine and farming. He had 460 scholars buried alive in a single grave. He organized people to build the Great Wall of China, but more than one million people died building it. •• Why was the first emperor thought to be a cruel tyrant? •• Why did he have 460 scholars killed?

Fast Forward

In 1974, three farmers began digging a well. A shovel hit something hard. Looking into the hole, they saw something made of baked clay. **A head appeared with eyes open, staring at them. The farmers reported their find.** •• What tells you the farmers had integrity?

Soon archaeologists arrived. They have spent over 30 years excavating 8,000 terra-cotta soldiers. **Each lifelike soldier has a unique face and expression.** •• How many soldiers have been excavated?

Over 8,000 clay soldiers stand guard over Qin's tomb.

Until 1974, no one knew of the massive underground army standing guard over the tomb of Qin Shi Huang. **Yet the army had been underfoot for more than 2,200 years.** The emperor's tomb remains untouched. It is 250 feet high and surrounded by a wall nearly four miles wide. No tomb has ever equaled that of the first emperor. **Over 700,000 workers are thought to have created Qin's tomb and his clay army.** •• Why is Qin's tomb considered the most impressive tomb ever built?

When the boy Qin came to the throne, he had three goals. **He wanted to conquer the other six kingdoms. He wanted to be the most powerful ruler in all of China. And he wanted to build the greatest tomb ever.** •• Do you think Qin accomplished his goals? •• Was he a good ruler? Why or why not?

CHAPTER FORTY-THREE

Buster and Homer

Narrative Fiction

Previously in the Third Quest

Buster and Homer were taken to the Quest Central lab. In a flash, the two famous robots found an error in the code. With a keystroke, Lambert was transported to the year 2300. Dr. X thought Lambert needed time to grow up. He wasn't ready to be a Quest leader, not yet. •• What evidence in the text tells why Lambert was returned to the year 2300?

• • •

The Important When: The year 2300 CE
The Important Where: Lambert's house

Suitcases sat by the door. Lambert's parents walked through the empty house. Buster's screen was blank, and Lambert's room was spotless. •• Why is Buster's screen blank?

Mr. and Mrs. Walker took their bags to their room and began unpacking. They weren't worried about Lambert, but they did wonder why his room was so clean.

A door slammed. The Walkers heard Lambert's footsteps on the stairs. He was wearing a yellow baseball cap and balancing a large, ugly frog on one hand. •• What text evidence verifies that Lambert had been on the Quest?

• • •

The Important Where: Quest Central
•• What is the important "when"?

In the lab, Buster and Homer were working to get Ling, Anna, Tuppins, Shack, and Zack to the same time and place.

Dr. Kumar and Dr. X stood in a corner talking quietly. Dr. Kumar stroked his chin. "Homer and Buster are brilliant. What a shame they were hidden so long."

Dr. X said, "Finally, they can show the world what advanced androids can do. Their creator was forced to retire after the Quest 2200 team was lost. The whole X-2200 project was shut down."

Dr. Popov overheard their conversation and said, "The robots are impressive, but they should not be trusted. We do not know who was responsible for the lost team. It may have been the androids. They should be watched, and watched carefully." •• Why does Dr. Popov think the androids should be watched?

Dr. X ignored Dr. Popov. He was clearly prejudiced against the androids. Dr. X summarized what the androids had accomplished and what they would do next. "Buster and Homer scanned thousands of lines of code. They found the error — the human error — and fixed it. Lambert is home already. It won't be much longer before the team is back in one place and time."

Dr. Popov said, "Buster and Homer's human traits are a problem. They got distracted. They are too human." •• What evidence in the text explains why Dr. Popov doesn't trust the robots?

Dr. Kumar looked at Dr. Popov and hesitated. Then he said, "We need the robots. We can't lose another team. Dr. Popov, you will follow my directions and leave the robots to their work." •• What evidence in the text suggests that Dr. Kumar doesn't trust Dr. Popov?

• • •

The Important When: The year 2300
The Important Where: The decrepit school

A minute before the bell rang, Lambert walked through the door. Mindy and Kate jumped up and gave him a hug. The class snickered, but then everyone started talking to Lambert. Melvin said, "Hey, Lambert, that mummy stuff was cool." •• What do you think the class thinks about Lambert now?

Mindy stood behind Lambert, staring intently at his baseball cap. Mindy tugged on Lambert's sweater and whispered, "Lambert, where did you get that cap?"

Ms. X was staring at the yellow cap, too. It had a small Quest logo on the back. Ms. X was thinking about the year 2200. They had all been given different-colored baseball caps. Bella's cap had been purple. •• Who is Bella? •• Listen to the paragraph again. What questions do you have?

Ms. X stared at the cap and the giant frog sitting at Lambert's feet. Without thinking, Ms. X picked up *Beelzebufo* and wondered, "Could Lambert have discovered the missing team?"

Five holograms suddenly appeared, walking together. A huge building could be seen on a hill in the distance. Ms. X thought, "Good for Buster and Homer." •• What had the androids accomplished?

Ms. X looked for Lambert. He was huddled in a corner with Mindy and Kate. •• What do you think is happening with Mindy, Kate, and Lambert?

CHAPTER FORTY-FOUR

Ancient Civilizations and Religions

Informational

Introduction

The great civilizations had many things in common. People farmed. They had irrigation systems and extra food to store and trade. People stopped being nomads. Instead of moving around in search of food, people built villages and cities. People had different jobs, and governments were formed. •• Why do you think governments were formed?

Each of the early civilizations also had a writing system. People kept records, wrote about their lives, and created artwork. •• What are four things the great civilizations had in common?

Religions

Every great civilization also had a religion. Stories about the gods and goddesses helped explain what the people didn't understand. •• What did the stories about the gods and goddesses explain?

Religion in Mesopotamian

In Mesopotamia, each city had its own god. The gods were shown in human form. The Sumerians believed people were created to serve the gods. They built great temples and sacrificed animals to the gods. The Sumerians thought the gods gave people prosperity on Earth and in the afterlife.
•• Listen to the last sentence again. What do you think "prosperity on Earth" means?

Ziggurat (temple to the gods) in Ur

Religion in Ancient Egypt

The ancient Egyptians believed in thousands of gods and goddesses. The gods and goddesses were often shown as part human and part animal. As part of their religion, the ancient Egyptians also practiced magic. The Egyptians treasured their spells and potions.

After death, the Egyptians believed they would be judged by the god Osiris. **If the judgment was good, the person was happy. If the judgment was bad, the person was eaten by a monster!**
•• Describe the ancient Egyptian religion.

Egyptian art showing Osiris

Egyptian temple of Karnak in Luxor

Religion in the Indus Valley

By observing artifacts, historians hypothesize that the people prayed to a Mother Goddess. Evidence has also been found of a male god who has three faces. This god is similar to a Hindu god worshipped by many people today.

Unlike other civilizations, the people of the Indus Valley did not worship their gods by building temples. Instead, they may have had bathing rituals dedicated to the Mother Goddess. •• How was the Indus Valley religion different from Mesopotamia and Egypt?

Three-faced figure, Indus Valley artifact

Religion in Ancient China

In ancient China, people worshipped their ancestors, spirits, and gods. They also believed in an afterlife. However, because the people were often at war, they began to question their beliefs. They wondered why the ancestors and spirits didn't bring them peace. •• What made the people of China question their religion?

A man named Confucius (551 BCE–479 BCE) became a great thinker and teacher. **Confucius believed that a good life was not the will of the gods. He believed humans could tell right from wrong. He also believed that people, not the gods, were responsible for making the world perfect.** Confucius taught people to become well educated. **He said people should work to be good, honor the family, and respect order.** •• What did Confucius teach?

When Qin came to power, Confucius had already died. **Emperor Qin told his people that he was "all-mighty heaven."** **Qin had followers of Confucius killed because they were scholars and did not worship him.** •• What evidence in the text explains why Qin killed Confucius' followers?

Confucius lived about 2,500 years ago, but people throughout the world know his sayings. •• Who do you think had the greater impact on the world, Qin or Confucius?

Confucius

Conclusion

The great ancient civilizations had much in common. A central part of each civilization was religion. Each religion helped people explain why things happened.

CHAPTER FORTY-FIVE

Transported

Narrative Fiction

Previously in the Third Quest

Like mad scientists, Homer and Buster were intently scanning thousands of lines of code. They were working to bring Ling, Anna, Tuppins, Shack, and Zack to one location and one time.

Mindy, Lambert, and Kate were huddled together in the old decrepit classroom. Mindy had observed a Quest logo on Lambert's baseball cap. •• What hypothesis do you have about the baseball cap?

• • •

The Important When: The year 2300 CE
The Important Where: Mindy's home

Mindy had always been busy with school activities. Since returning from the Quest, she had dropped all extra activities. She went to school. She hung out with Lambert and Kate. After school, she went home and then went straight to her bedroom.

Mindy's mother knocked lightly on Mindy's door. She sat on Mindy's bed and said, "You are pretty miserable, aren't you?"

Mindy nodded.

Mindy's mom said, "I think your dad and I made a mistake." •• What text evidence supports Mrs. Herzig's conclusion that Mindy is miserable?

Mindy's eyes glistened. Her mom said, "I will make it right. Please be careful." Then she gave Mindy a hug.

Mindy said, "I just need to finish the Quest. Then I'll be back. I need to be with my team."

Mrs. Herzig smiled. "I understand." Then, without hesitating, she went to the den and logged into Quest Central's parent website. A big, ugly frog sat at Mrs. Herzig's feet. Mrs. Herzig smiled at the frog and said, "Thank you. I need moral support." •• The text doesn't explain, but why do you think Mrs. Herzig needs moral support?

Then Mrs. Herzig clicked a link and said, "Hello. This is Mrs. Bonnie Herzig. I would like to give my permission for Mindy Herzig to return to the 2300 team."

• • •

The Important When: 100 BCE, about 2,000 years ago
The Important Where: Ancient Greece

In the blink of an eye, Mindy found herself sitting on a hill. Tuppins walked up the hill and sat next to her. His unsettled feeling went away. Mindy smiled and said, "So, Tuppins, where are we?"

Tuppins pointed at a huge monument that loomed in the distance. Mindy recognized it. At ten, she had visited the ancient ruins with her parents. A faint smile crossed Tuppins' face as he said, "It would appear that we are in **ancient Greece.**" •• What evidence in the text indicates that Tuppins is happy to see Mindy?

Anna, Ling, Zack, and Shack all came running. When they reached the top of the hill, there was quite a commotion. Shack whooped when he saw Mindy and the others. Ling and Anna couldn't stop talking, asking questions, and hugging their friends. Zack nodded at Mindy and gave her a thumbs-up. In a strong and confident voice, Zack said, "You and the *Beelzebufo* are good omens." •• What does Zack's confidence predict?

Mindy thought, "Zack sounds like himself again."

• • •

Dr. X watched as the team of six was reunited. She smiled. Buster and Homer had proved themselves. They

were the world's best programmers. •• What event supports Dr. X's conclusion that Homer and Buster were the world's best programmers?

Dr. X was optimistic. This team would prove itself and return to the year 2300 unharmed and confident. Their future was promising. •• Use information from the text and earlier chapters to explain why Dr. X is optimistic.

CHAPTER FORTY-SIX

The Golden Age of Greece
Informational

Ancient Greece (500 BCE to 146 BCE)

Ancient Greece was located on a peninsula across the Mediterranean Sea from Africa. •• Find Africa on the map. Point to the Mediterranean Sea. Now find ancient Greece.

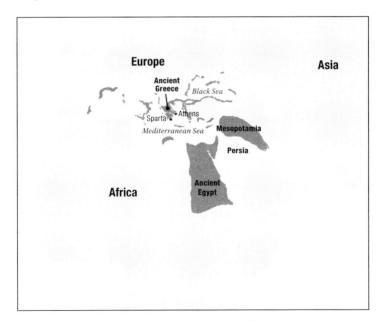

Ancient Greece and Greek settlements

The Greek peninsula has many mountains, and the ground is rocky. Good farmland is scarce. To support their growing population, the Greeks turned to the sea.

Greek warship. The Greeks were great ship builders.

By about 500 BCE (2,500 years ago), there were more than 400 Greek settlements around the Mediterranean Sea and Black Sea. •• What text evidence explains why the Greeks moved into areas outside the Greek peninsula?

Greek City-States

The Greek settlements developed into city-states. The city-states shared a language and religion, but the armies, customs, and governments of each city-state were different. Greece was not peaceful. The city-states were often at war with each other. •• Use evidence from the paragraph above to describe the city-states.

The Olympic Games

Every four years, a truce was held. All fighting stopped. Instead of fighting, the city-states held athletic games. These were the world's first Olympic Games.

The Greek city-states sent their best athletes to Olympia, Greece, to compete. There were feasts, celebrations, and athletic contests. The ancient Olympic Games were held for over 1,000 years. (About 200 years ago, the modern Olympic Games renewed the tradition.) •• Where were the Olympics first held? •• What questions do you have about these first Olympics?

Athens, Greece

Athens was one of the most important city-states in Greece. The city was protected by the goddess of wisdom and warfare.

Goddess of wisdom and military might

For ten years, from 490–480 BCE, all of Greece fought a war with Persia (modern-day Iran). Athens won the war and forced the other city-states to pay them fees. The upper class in Athens became very wealthy.

After the war, the leaders in Athens gave people a say in government. This was the world's first democracy. Every free male over 18 who had parents born in Athens was allowed to vote. The men voted on important matters and elected their generals. •• Who was allowed to vote? •• Who was not allowed to vote? •• How were men and women treated differently in Athens?

Athens also became the home of great thinkers. Socrates, Plato, and Aristotle were all Greek thinkers who people study today. These thinkers and teachers asked questions such as "What is good?" and "What is evil?"

Greek thinking formed the beginning of scientific thinking. The Greeks asked questions and looked for answers to mysteries through observation, facts (or evidence), and logic. The Greeks made advances in mathematics, astronomy, and medicine. They could even calculate the distance from the moon to Earth. Two thousand, five hundred years later, we still use classic Greek mathematical formulas, and college students and scholars study ancient Greek thinking. •• What text evidence tells you why the Greek thinkers were important to the modern world?

The Temple of Hephaestus in Athens, Greece, is an example of classical Greek architecture.

•• What did the modern world inherit from the ancient Greeks?

CHAPTER FORTY-SEVEN

The Olympics
Narrative Fiction

Previously in the Third Quest

The androids had transported Anna, Ling, Zack, Shack, and Tuppins to ancient Greece. With her mother's permission, Mindy had joined them. •• Where is the team now? •• How did Mindy get reunited with the team?

• • •

The Important When: 100 BCE, about 2,000 years ago
The Important Where: Olympia, Greece

The kids were busy catching up. Shack said, "Hey, curly-haired girl. How'd you get back?"

Mindy said, "Mom could see I needed to be here with you. Sometimes, Quest let us view your holograms. I tried to view you on the web, but we weren't given access very often."

Ling said, "I knew we were being watched."

Mindy said, "You, we ... are celebrities. Everyone knows who we are."

Shack said, "So the parents are all good then. I can hear them saying, 'You can do it. Finish the Quest. Come back the victors!'" •• From Shack's pep talk, what do you know about Shack and his family?

Zack looked at Shack. Zack wondered if Shack knew about his parents' arrest. If he did, Shack had never said anything. Shack was an asset — upbeat, positive, supportive. •• From Zack's point of view, what do you know about Shack? •• What does Zack need to overcome?

Before long, a crowd was pushing the kids along toward a stadium. Anna, Ling, and Mindy found themselves sitting on a grassy slope with forty thousand other spectators. People stood up and began leaving. Whatever had been happening was over.

Tup joined the girls. He was happy and launched into a soliloquy. "We have arrived at the Olympic Games. The games are being held to celebrate the god Zeus.

"The Olympic Games were played for over a thousand years, until the Romans conquered the Greeks. Because the Roman emperors had become Christians, they forbade the games to continue. The Romans did not want celebrations honoring Zeus to continue. The Romans wanted to eliminate the worship of Greek gods and goddesses." •• What text evidence explains why the ancient Olympic Games were discontinued for over 1,000 years?

Ling smiled at Tuppins and said, "Hey, Tup. Do you know what's happened to the rest of the team?" Tuppins looked confused.

Mindy said, "You know — Zack and Shack?"

Tuppins said, "Tomorrow is the second day of the games. There will be events. Then on the third day, there will be a feast in honor of Zeus. One hundred cows will be killed."

The girls waited patiently until Tup finally answered the question. "On the fourth day, Shack will wrestle and I will be in a footrace. Only the best may compete." •• Why did the girls wait patiently for an answer to Ling's question? •• What will Tuppins and Shack do on the fourth day of the games?

Shack and Zack were walking up the grassy slope to join them. Anna noticed Zack had a whip in his hand. "Tup, why does Zack have a whip?"

Tuppins said, "If someone does not follow the rules, he can be whipped by a judge." Anna raised her eyebrows. •• What is Zack's new role? •• Why are the girls simply spectators?

• • •

The Important When: 2300 CE
The Important Where: Quest Central

Dr. Kumar asked Dr. X to meet him in his office. He was staring at a map. "The team is in classical Greece. If all goes well, they should proceed to Rome and then follow migration patterns to Australia and the Americas."

Dr. X said, "It's too risky. The team needs to return soon."

Dr. Kumar said, "I agree. I haven't decided when yet, but soon." Then Dr. Kumar hesitated and said, "Bella, I have something for you to think about . . ."

Dr. X was puzzled. She thought, "No one calls me by my first name." •• What is Dr. X (aka Ms. X's) first name?

Dr. Kumar said, "With the androids back, we may be able to return you to your team, but you must think clearly about the consequences." •• This is an interesting turn of events. What can you conclude about Dr. X? •• What text evidence from this chapter and previous chapters leads to your conclusion?

CHAPTER FORTY-EIGHT

The Competition

Narrative Fiction

Previously in the Third Quest

The team of six was in ancient Greece. Tuppins and Shack were set to compete, and Zack would judge the events. •• What are Zack and Shack competing in? •• What have you learned about the ancient Olympic Games so far?

The mystery continues, but answers are near. Dr. Kumar asked Dr. Bella X (aka Ms. X) if she would like to rejoin her Quest 2200 team.

• • •

The Important When: The year 2300

The Important Where: Ms. X's home

Ms. X (aka Dr. X) sat motionless at her computer. Her lavender baseball cap hung on the wall behind her. She had a lot to consider. She was 115 years old. The last time she had seen her team was in the year 2200. She had been just fifteen. Dr. X began a list of questions:

1. Where is the Quest 2200 team?
2. What year are they traveling in?
3. How old are my team members now?

•• What other questions do you think Dr. X should ask?

• • •

The Important When: 100 BCE

The Important Where: Olympia, Greece

Once again, Anna, Ling, and Mindy were sitting on the grassy slope — reduced to being spectators. Anna said, "I wish we could compete." •• Why are the girls sidelined?

Anna asked, "Ling, does Tuppins run track at home?"

Ling said, "He does. He is one of the top runners in the state. I don't think he cares if he wins or loses. Once he hears the starting gun, he runs like the wind. Tuppins rarely loses."

Anna said, "A new side of Tuppins! That's cool. He kind of grows on you, doesn't he?" Ling nodded. •• What text evidence tells you something new about Tuppins? •• What does "He kind of grows on you" mean?

The girls watched as Tuppins raced the length of the stadium — once, twice, three times . . . sixteen times. Some of the runners were tiring, but not Tuppins. Only one other runner was keeping pace with him. Then a stumble. The crowd gasped.

One racer finished lengths ahead of the other racers. The winner's name was announced. Tuppins! A palm leaf was placed in his hand. Everyone clapped. The spectators threw flowers to Tuppins and tied a red ribbon around his head. Anna, Mindy, and Ling could hardly contain themselves. •• What text evidence demonstrates how the travelers have become a team?

The girls strained to see the next event — boxing. The competitors were huge men. They had massive shoulders, arms, and fists. Their noses were crooked and their faces were scarred and lumpy. Anna asked, "Why is Shack there?" Someone was wrapping leather straps around his hands.

Tuppins joined the girls. Mindy said, "Tuppins, it looks like Shack is going to box. He was supposed to wrestle."

Tuppins said, "There are no weight classes and no rules in boxing. It is said that boxing was brutal and the outcome often gruesome. Men were known to die." •• Are the facts about boxing relevant? How so?

Mindy said, "We can't leave Shack there." The travelers stood up but didn't know what to do. Just then, Zack walked into the stadium. He talked with the men and pointed at Shack. Then Zack took Shack's arm and escorted him away.

The team walked calmly away from the crowds. They hoped Shack and Zack would do the same. It wasn't long before the boys joined Tuppins, Mindy, Anna, and Ling.

They all kept walking. They didn't want to be noticed. Finally, when they were away from the crowds, they stopped and rested under a tree. Zack said, "The rules are clear. To compete in the Olympics, you have to be born here. As a judge, I was able to disqualify Shack."

Shack grinned. "Those boxing dudes looked mean. I'm glad to be a foreigner here." •• What evidence in the previous paragraph tells you what a foreigner is?

Mindy looked at Zack. She appreciated his logic. He was back to being himself. •• Zack's character has evolved. Use evidence in the text to describe Zack now.

Mindy found herself carrying the *Beelzebufo*. He had an orange folder in his mouth.

• • •

The Important When: 2300 CE
The Important Where: The old decrepit school

The holograms of the Quest 2300 team appeared. Mindy was back with the team in ancient Greece. Melvin said, "Hey, the frog is back with them. That's a good omen." •• In this paragraph, what does "that's a good omen" mean?

Lambert said, "The team has passed another test."
Kate said, "I hope they will be back soon."

Ms. X handed out an assignment, but she didn't say anything. Ms. X seemed distracted. •• Why do you think Ms. X is distracted? •• Predict what you think Ms. X will decide to do by voting.

CHAPTER FORTY-NINE

Athens and Sparta

Informational

Previously Learned

The city-states in ancient Greece had a language and religion in common, but each city-state had its own customs, governments, and armies. These city-states were often at war with each other. •• By looking at the picture, what observations can you make about the ancient Greeks?

Scene from ancient Greece on black figure pottery

Introduction

Even though the city-states were often at war with each other, they viewed the rest of the world as barbaric and uncivilized. Two of the most powerful of these city-states were Athens and Sparta.

Athens

Because Athens won the war with Persia, the other city-states paid Athens fees or taxes. Athens became rich and powerful. Almost every free man owned slaves. The people of Athens had time to think, study, build great temples, and invent new ways of doing things. •• Explain why the people of Athens had extra time to invent new ways of doing things.

Government

By about 440 BCE, the people of Athens had developed the world's first democracy. If you were a male and born in Athens, you had a say in the way the city-state was run. •• Who determined how to run the city-state?

All males over the age of 18 voted. Meetings took place every 10 days. It was the duty of male citizens to go to the meetings. For a vote to take place, there had to be 6,000 citizens at the meeting. All free males had a voice in the laws and how Athens was run.

Whether rich or poor, any citizen who wished to speak before a vote could. •• Explain how democracy in Athens worked.

The Arts and Sciences

The government in Athens encouraged people to be artists, scientists, and thinkers. Today, people still read the writings of the ancient Greeks. Actors still perform ancient Greek plays. Students, engineers, and carpenters still use math that the Greeks developed. •• What evidence supports the conclusion that the ancient Athenians were successful?

Growing Up in Athens

Boys and girls were taught at home until the age of six. Then boys went to school. They learned to read and write. They studied the arts, sciences, and math. At eighteen, the boys went to military school. •• Describe the life of a boy in Athens.

Girls did not attend school. If their mothers could read and write, the girls learned at home. Girls in Athens learned skills like spinning and cooking. They were trained to spend most of their time at home. They were allowed to leave the house only to perform religious duties. •• Describe the life of a girl in Athens.

Sparta

Just one hundred miles from Athens was the city-state of Sparta. Sparta had no great public buildings — just simple houses. Sparta was made up of land that had been won from other people. The people who had been conquered were called helots. The helots were slaves to the Spartans. They farmed the land and did all the hard labor. •• Who were the helots?

Spartan males were not allowed to farm, trade, or have a profession. Instead, all Spartan males were soldiers. Their only jobs were to keep

Statue of Leonidas, warrior and Spartan king

the helots under control and to go to war with other city-states. •• If you were a male citizen in Sparta, what would your job be? •• Who did all the other work?

Government

Unlike Athens, Sparta was not a democracy, so no one voted. Sparta was ruled by two kings and the military.

The Arts and Sciences

The military government frowned on the arts, sciences, and thinking. •• Describe how Sparta was different than Athens.

Growing Up in Sparta

If a male baby was small and sickly, the child was left on a mountainside to die. At the age of seven, boys were sent to live in military schools. They learned that the state was more important than their families. They learned to persevere through hunger and pain. They learned how to attack and fight to the death. All Spartan males were trained to be full-time soldiers. •• Describe the life of a Spartan boy.

In Sparta, the girls went to school from the age of seven. They learned to read and write. They were encouraged to exercise and play athletic games because the Spartans wanted healthy mothers. •• Describe the life of a Spartan girl. •• Share whether you would choose to live in Athens or Sparta by voting. Explain your vote.

Greek Religion and Myths
Informational

Despite their differences, the ancient Greeks all shared a religion. The people believed in twelve great gods and goddesses. All twelve gods and goddesses lived on Mount Olympus. Zeus was the king of the gods and the ruler of sky and Earth. •• Even though the ancient Greeks had many differences, what did they all share?

Many myths about the Greek gods were told from one generation to another. A myth teaches a lesson or explains something in nature. •• What is the reason for myths?

Prometheus and the Gift of Fire
In the beginning, Earth had no living creatures. Zeus commanded that the gods Epimetheus (ep-i-MEE-thee-us) and Prometheus (pro-MEE-thee-us) fill the Earth's vast empty spaces with living things.

The gods followed Zeus' orders. They filled the land, sea, and air with animals. •• What did Zeus order Epimetheus and Prometheus to do?

Epimetheus gave the creatures claws and sharp teeth.

He gave the creatures size, strength, and speed.

Prometheus soon realized there were no gifts left for man. Epimetheus had given all the gifts away, so man was left without protection. Prometheus was worried. How would man protect himself? •• Use text evidence to explain why Prometheus was worried about man.

Prometheus knew the gift of fire remained. Man would be all-powerful with fire. Zeus said that man should never have fire. Fire would make man too much like the gods. •• Why did Zeus want to keep fire from man?

Prometheus could not leave man helpless. He hesitated, but then he disobeyed Zeus. He stole a lightning bolt from Zeus and gave it to man. •• How did Prometheus help man?

Just as Zeus had predicted, with fire man became all-powerful. Fire gave man tools. With fire, man learned how to make tools for farming and building. Fire also gave man the ability to make dangerous weapons for hunting and war. Fire gave man great strength. •• Describe how fire made man powerful.

Zeus looked down at Earth and could see fire glowing. Zeus grew angry. Zeus knew that Prometheus had disobeyed him.

As a consequence, Zeus banished Prometheus to a mountaintop. Zeus made the god helpless. He chained Prometheus to a rock where the hot sun burned his skin and harsh storms beat against him. •• What lesson does this myth teach about disobeying the gods? •• What does the myth explain about man?

Pandora's Jar

Man had accepted the gift of fire. After chaining Prometheus to a rock, Zeus needed a punishment for man. •• What lesson do you think this myth will teach man?

Zeus ordered the god of craftsmen and sculptors to create the first woman. Zeus named the woman Pandora. The woman was sent to Epimetheus as a gift. Pandora was beautiful and charming, and she became Epimetheus' wife.

Zeus gave Pandora a large pottery jar and told her that she must never open the jar. •• What was Zeus' instruction?

For a long time, Pandora followed Zeus' order. Then one day, when her husband was away, Pandora's curiosity got the best of her. She thought she could just take a look. •• What do you think "got the best of her" means?

Pandora slowly lifted the lid of the pottery jar. When she did that, ten thousand horrors were released — pain, disease, war, and death. Pandora tried to close the lid, but it was too late. •• What happened when Pandora opened the jar?

Only one thing saved mankind. Hope was left in the jar.

•• What has saved man from all the horrors of pain, disease, war, and death?

Afterword

NOTE: Today, a common saying is: *Don't open Pandora's box.* •• What do you think that means? •• Why do you think the saying is relevant today?

CHAPTER FIFTY-ONE

Alexander the Great

Informational

Previously Learned

The city-states of Greece shared a language and a religion, but they were often at war with one another. They viewed the rest of the world as barbaric or uncivilized.
•• How did the Greeks view the rest of the world?

From 490 to 480 BCE, all of Greece had fought a war with the enemy empire of Persia. Athens won the war and forced the other Greek city-states to pay them taxes. •• Why was Athens able to force the other Greek city-states to pay them taxes?

War Between Sparta and Athens

After the war with Persia, Athens and Sparta also agreed to a thirty-year peace. As Athens became stronger and wealthier, the Spartans became jealous. In 431 BCE, Sparta declared war on Athens. •• Why did Sparta declare war on Athens?

A long and brutal war followed. After 27 years, Sparta finally defeated Athens, but the city-states were left weak and exhausted. The Golden Age of Greece had ended. •• Use text evidence to explain what caused the demise of the Golden Age of Greece.

Macedonia

To the north of Greece lay Macedonia. The people of Macedonia lived in tribes and were ruled by warlord-like rulers. The people of Macedonia thought they were Greek citizens, but the Greeks saw them as barbarians. •• Why do you think the Macedonians were seen as barbarians?

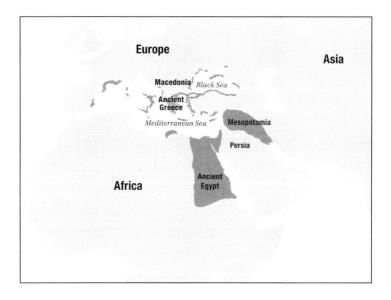

King Philip of Macedonia

In 359 BCE, Philip II came to the throne. He wanted respect for Macedonia, so he built the best-equipped and best-trained army in the region. With his powerful army, Philip began conquering the Greek city-states.

By 338 BCE, King Philip had crushed most of the Greeks and forced the city-states to live in peace. By doing this, Philip accomplished what the Greeks had never been able to do. King Philip of Macedonia united Greece. •• What were the great accomplishments of King Philip II?

Next, King Philip was determined to defeat Greece's enemy to the east — Persia. But King Philip was assassinated. Upon his death, his twenty-year-old son, Alexander, became King Alexander of Macedonia. •• What stopped King Philip from going to war and defeating Persia?

Alexander the Great

After establishing his own power in Greece, Alexander led the Macedonian armies into Persia. By the age of 23, Alexander had defeated the Persians and taken another title — the Great King of Persia. Not satisfied, Alexander went on to conquer Egypt. In Egypt, he became a pharaoh. •• Describe how Alexander not only inherited his father's power but also became even more powerful.

Alexander became known as Alexander the Great. As he conquered other lands, he spread Greek culture throughout Europe, the Middle East, and Northern Africa. •• What did Alexander accomplish?

By 326 BCE, at the age of 30 and still not satifisfied, Alexander led his army into India. Victorious but exhausted, Alexander's army finally said they would go no further. Alexander had no choice. He began the journey home, but fell ill and died at the age of 32. •• Why did Alexander's army refuse to go farther?

The world sees Alexander as one of the world's greatest generals. He was well educated, intelligent, and courageous. Historians also see a dark side. Alexander was known to have murdered close advisors and friends. Thousands of people were killed after his conquests. Evidence even suggests that Alexander may have been part of his father's assassination. •• Describe Alexander's dark side. •• Vote on whether Alexander was great or not. Be prepared to explain your vote or opinion.

After Alexander's death, Greece became divided again as Alexander's generals fought for power. By 146 BCE, Greece was defeated by the Romans and absorbed into the mighty Roman Empire. •• By about 2,100 years ago, what was the fate of the Greeks?

Afterword

The ancient civilizations have a long history of wars. Before the defeat of Persia, the Greek city-states were often at war with each other.

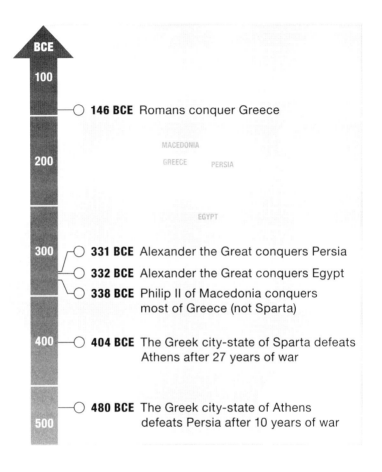

BCE

100

○ **146 BCE** Romans conquer Greece

MACEDONIA

GREECE   PERSIA

200

EGYPT

300

○ **331 BCE** Alexander the Great conquers Persia

○ **332 BCE** Alexander the Great conquers Egypt

○ **338 BCE** Philip II of Macedonia conquers
most of Greece (not Sparta)

400 ─○ **404 BCE** The Greek city-state of Sparta defeats
Athens after 27 years of war

○ **480 BCE** The Greek city-state of Athens
defeats Persia after 10 years of war

500

CHAPTER FIFTY-TWO

The Decision

Narrative Fiction

Previously in the Third Quest

The Third Quest 2300 team was together in ancient Greece. Tuppins had won an Olympic track event. Shack had been rescued from a boxing match that could have killed him. Zack had used logic to escort Shack away from danger.

Dr. Bella X (aka Ms. X) had a decision to make. Dr. Kumar thought she could be reunited with her team. •• What team did Dr. X belong to?

• • •

Dr. X was at Quest Central with Dr. Kumar. She said, "Before I decide anything, I need to make sure the Quest 2300 team is safe. I believe they've demonstrated perseverance, teamwork, and integrity. With one more transport — to Rome — I believe we will be clear about the traits that will ensure their future successes."

Dr. Kumar said, "I agree." After a pause, he said, "Bella, we believe the Quest 2200 team is in Rome. Homer and

Buster are going to try to place the Quest 2300 team in the same place and time." Dr. X looked intently at Dr. Kumar, but didn't say anything. •• Put yourself in Dr. X's shoes. What do you think she is thinking? •• What do you think Dr. X should do — stay, wait and go later, or go? •• Why do you think the authors wrote this chapter?

An Impending Decision

Narrative Fiction

Previously in the Third Quest

Homer and Buster were trying to determine how to bring the Quest 2200 and 2300 teams together in ancient Rome.

• • •

The Important Where: Quest Central

The Important When: The year 2300

Dr. Kumar said, "Bella, if Homer and Buster can bring the teams together, you may need to join your team in a few hours."

Dr. X paused and said, "I still have many questions."

Dr. Kumar said, "Send me your questions. I will do my best to get you answers quickly."

Dr. X nodded. She was usually confident, but this was different. Dr. X sat down at her computer and tried to think clearly. Her list of questions already included:

1.   Where is the Quest 2200 team?

2. What year are they traveling in?

3. How old are the team members now?

Dr. X typed:

4. If I go, how old will I be? •• How old do you think Dr. X will be — 15 or 115?

5. Will the team recognize me?

6. Will we be able to return?

7. If yes, will we return to our homes in the year 2200?

8. If no, what will happen to us?

Dr. X sighed as she thought about her life in the year 2300. She wondered what would happen to her class if she left. She knew Kate and Lambert would be fine. Lambert had shown no signs of bullying anyone. In fact, he had become the class scholar — helping other students study for quizzes. •• Describe how Lambert's character has evolved.

Beelzebufo appeared at Dr. X's feet. Dr. X relaxed and chuckled. She realized in that moment that she had made her decision. Thinking wasn't going to change anything. Ms. X shrugged her shoulders. At 115 years old, why not? •• What is Dr. X's decision? What text evidence leads you to that conclusion?

• • •

The Important Where: Ancient Rome
The Important When: Between 100 BCE and 400 CE

The Quest 2300 team found themselves walking through
an open-air market. Mindy laughed, "Ah, transported again
and all accounted for."

Shack said, "A smooth transport . . . they must be getting
their act together at Quest Central." •• What evidence does
Shack have to support this conclusion?

Tuppins said, "We are no longer in Greece. In most of
the Greek city-states, women from wealthier homes were
not allowed to go out, except during religious events like
the Olympics. Slaves did whatever was needed outside the
home."

Zack smiled and said, "Women's rights have clearly moved forward." Several men in togas were walking into a large building. Zack said, "Rome?"

Tuppins said, "Women could be seen in public in Rome, but they could not own property or vote." •• Today, women have more rights than women in ancient Rome. What are two rights modern-day women have that Roman women did not?

Five teenagers stood near the entrance of a library. They were dressed like everyone else, but somehow they seemed out of place. Before Tuppins could say more, Anna, observant as ever, pointed at one of the kid's hands. He held a gray baseball cap. •• Anna continues to be an asset. What text evidence supports that conclusion? Why is the baseball cap an important clue?

• • •

The Important Where: Quest Central
The Important When: The year 2300

Dr. X opened Dr. Kumar's email and read, "Bella, here are the answers to some of your questions. There are many unknowns; however, Buster and Homer have managed to get the Quest 2200 and Quest 2300 teams in the same location and time. As soon as you've read this, please join us in the lab." Dr. X quickly scanned the email.

1. Where is the Quest 2200 team? (Rome)
2. What year are they traveling in? (We think they are somewhere between 100 BCE and 400 CE.)
3. How old are the 2200 team members now? (still 15)

4. If I go, how old will I be? (We don't know.)

5. Will the team recognize me? (We don't know.)

6. Will we be able to return? (No, you will not be able to return. To the world, the Quest 2200 team is lost in the past. We cannot change history.)

7. If yes, will we return to our homes in the year 2200? (You will not return.)

8. If no, what will happen to us? (We think the team will continue traveling forward, but we are not certain.) •• Use text evidence to support Dr. Kumar's observation that there are many unknowns.

Dr. X quickly opened her computer and wrote to each student. Minutes later, she shut her computer down and headed toward the lab. The *Beelzebufo*'s head stuck out of a backpack on her back. •• What do you think Dr. X wrote to her students? •• What do you think the *Beelzebufo* foreshadows, or predicts?

CHAPTER FIFTY-FOUR

When in Rome

Narrative Fiction

Previously in the Third Quest

Dr. X wrote to her students at the decrepit school and then went to the lab. She was ready to rejoin the lost 2200 team, but there were many unanswered questions. Both Quest teams were in Rome.

• • •

The Important Where: Ancient Rome
The Important When: Between 100 BCE and 400 CE

A group of five teens stood near the entrance of a library. One of the kids held a gray baseball cap. Before anyone could say anything, the group of five teenagers disappeared in the crowded street. •• Who were the five teenagers?

The Quest 2300 team quickly spread out in twos looking for the lost team. They had to connect! A half hour later, Mindy and Tuppins sat at the base of a beautiful marble fountain waiting for the others. They'd found no sign of the missing team. Tuppins was talking.

"There is some evidence that at one time, ancient Rome had 28 libraries, 19 aqueducts, 46,602 apartment blocks, 1,790 great houses, 290 granaries, 856 baths, 254 bakeries, 144 public bathrooms, some number of temples . . ." **Tuppins paused and muttered, "Missing data." Then he continued, "And a million people."** •• In ancient times, Rome was an advanced civilization. What evidence does Tuppins provide to support this conclusion?

Mindy was always in awe of Tuppins' mastery of facts but was distracted wondering about the lost team. She said, "So, what did you say about bathrooms?"

Tuppins said, "The Romans had toilets and sewage systems that carried away the waste." At that, Mindy started to smile, but Tuppins was on a roll. "There's been evidence that the public bathrooms were quite unsanitary. Two thousand years ago, the Romans were an advanced civilization, but they had no knowledge of germs. The sewers were inhabited by rats. Actually, the city is said to have been crawling with rats."

Under normal circumstances, Mindy would have asked about the rats, but she was only half listening — wondering if they would find the Quest 2200 team. Mindy scanned the crowded street. On a paved walkway, Zack and Ling were walking toward them. She could barely see Anna and Shack also heading toward the fountain.

Zack and Ling walked silently toward the fountain, but Shack and Anna broke into a sprint. Out of breath, Anna told the others, "They are going to a bathhouse not far from here. We couldn't catch up to them without separating, so we came back for you."

The six team members huddled. Shack said, "The bath-house has separate entrances for the men and women."

Anna muttered, "At least they let the women in."

Ling was quiet. Then she said, "Zack and I have been talking. Do you think the team knows they're lost? They look about the same age as their photos. If we find them, what do we say?"

The group grew quiet as they pondered the question. What do you say to people who have been lost for a hundred years? •• What would you say? •• What do you want to find out before the story concludes?

Do as the Romans Do

Narrative Fiction

Previously in the Third Quest

The Quest 2300 team knew they had spotted the lost team. The baseball cap was the evidence.

The team spread out in twos trying to find the lost 2200 team. Shack and Anna spotted them outside a bathhouse. Ling and Zack wondered if the Quest 2200 team knew they were lost. Ling had asked, "If we find them, what do we say?" •• Why do you think Ling wondered what they should say to the team?

• • •

The Important Where: Ancient Rome
The Important When: Between 100 BCE and 400 CE

The 2300 team stood talking. Mindy said, "I forgot to tell you. Lambert came back from Emperor Qin's tomb with a baseball cap. It had a Quest 2200 logo on it." •• What can you conclude (or infer) from that information?

Zack said, "Let's find the 2200 team. We can figure out

what to say after we meet them."

Tuppins said, "The Roman baths were daily rituals for rich and poor alike. I believe we will find places to eat, socialize, exercise, and play sports. Then there will be a series of heated rooms and three grand pools with mosaic tiles. People cooled off in a cold bath, then relaxed in a warm bath, and then took a hot bath. It is said that they had to do things in a specific order."

Ling said, "We should go. If we don't find them before they enter the baths, we may lose them again." •• What text evidence led Ling to conclude that they should find the team before they enter the baths?

The Quest 2300 team hurried to the bathhouse. The 2200 team had separated and were moving toward different entrances. •• Why were they going to different entrances?

The girls hurried to the entrance where women and young girls were standing outside. Mindy, Ling, and Anna watched quietly as two girls suddenly ran over and hugged a third girl.

One of the girls said, "Bella, where have you been? What happened? Are you okay? We've been so worried about you." •• Who is Bella? •• How old do you think she is now?

Bella said, "I think I heard a loud crunching sound and then . . . I don't know what happened. How long have I been gone?"

One of the girls said, "Time is hard to judge. We were all working in Qin's tomb, crafting clay horses. Then we were transported to Greece, but you just vanished. We were afraid you had been left in the tomb." •• What do you think happened to Bella?

Mindy, Ling, and Anna walked over to the girls. Mindy said, "Hi. This is kind of strange, but we are a Quest team from the year 2300."

The other girls were quiet, and then one of them whispered, "Awesome. I'm Jasmine." •• Why were the girls quiet at first?

Another said, "And I'm Lani Smith."

The third girl said, "I'm Bella X."

As the others introduced themselves, Mindy stared at Bella. Then she realized that was rude. Finally, she said, "Bella, you look really familiar. Our teacher's last name was X. It's kind of an unusual name."

Bella smiled and said, "Your teacher? That's weird. Maybe it's just a coincidence." Then Bella paused. She looked confused, and so did Mindy. They were each trying to figure out why they seemed to know each other. •• What is confusing for the girls?

Anna asked the girls, "So where have you been?" They began talking about Siberia. No one had encountered humans, but both teams knew humans had been nearby. Gradually, their conversation grew animated.

They had a lot in common — a lot to talk about — but no one mentioned home. •• Describe what the girls have in common.

CHAPTER FIFTY-SIX

Remember My Words

Narrative Fiction

Previously in the Third Quest

Anna, Ling, and Mindy had introduced themselves to three members of the Quest 2200 team — Bella, Lani, and Jasmine. Bella had been reunited with the 2200 team but had no memory of her life as Dr. X. Bella X seemed oddly familiar to Mindy.

• • •

The Important Where: Ancient Rome
The Important When: Between 100 BCE and 400 CE

The six girls from the 2200 and 2300 teams waited for the boys outside the bathhouse. Soon the boys emerged. Barack broke into a huge smile, calling, "Hey, Bella! Where have you been?" Bella ran over and gave all three boys a hug.

When the commotion died down, Zack said, "Mindy, Ling, Anna. Meet Cody, Ronaldo, and Barack." There were smiles and polite conversation.

Bella picked up *Beelzebufo*. Cody turned to her and said,

"Hey, Bella and big frog, where have you been? Did you stay in the tombs? Did you find my cap?" Bella smiled and absentmindedly stroked *Beelzebufo* under his chin.

Before Bella could answer, Ronaldo said, "Bella, *Beelzebufo* is a good omen. I'm glad you're back. We need to stick together."

Jasmine said, "I can't wait to see where we go next. Now that Bella is here, I love the Quest. I hope it never ends!" Then she said, "Hey, maybe we can all travel together."

•• How does the dialogue support the conclusion that members of the Quest 2200 team are enjoying their travels?

Zack held up a white folder but before he could read it — poof. The 2200 team and the *Beelzebufo* vanished. •• Did you expect that to happen? What do you think happened to the 2200 team?

• • •

The Important Where: Quest Central
The Important When: Flashback to Bella's transport from the year 2300

Dr. Kumar looked at Dr. X. She nodded her consent. In the blink of an eye, Bella's young image appeared on the screen with Jasmine and Lani. The lab exploded into applause. •• Why did the lab explode into applause?

Homer and Buster were developing stellar reputations. Their skills and judgment were no longer questioned. Android prejudices were a thing of the past. •• How had Buster and Homer overcome human prejudices?

After Bella's transport, Dr. Kumar went to Dr. X's class. He raised his hand and waited. When the students quieted down, he said, "I have a story to tell you about Dr. X. It is an intriguing story."

Melvin said, "You mean Ms. X?"

Dr. Kumar said, "No, Dr. X is really a scientist from Quest Central, a senior scientist and traveler from the Quest 2200 team. A transporter error returned her to 2275 without her team. It has been difficult for her. Her team was lost. When she returned, 75 years had passed and her parents had died. All of a sudden, she was 90 years old." •• What evidence supports the conclusion that Bella X's transport to 2275 was difficult?

The class was quiet. Dr. Kumar continued, "We located the 2200 team, and Dr. X chose to rejoin them. You have folders on your desks. Dr. X wrote to each and every one of you. She asks that you read your memos and remember her words."

As Dr. Kumar left the room, a message appeared.

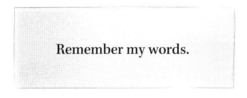

Remember my words.

•• Do you think the students will remember the lessons Ms. X taught them? What would Ms. X have said to you?

CHAPTER FIFTY-SEVEN

In Conclusion

Narrative Fiction

Illustration by Lucille Betti-Nash / Used with permission

Previously in the Third Quest

The two Quest teams from 2200 and 2300 had met in Rome. Both teams were intact. Then suddenly the 2200 team and *Beelzebufo* had disappeared.

• • •

Bewildered, everyone on the 2300 team was quiet. No one knew what to say or think. •• What do you think "bewildered" means?

Not sure what else to do, Zack opened the folder. After glancing at the memo inside, Zack said, "We're going home." •• How do you think the team feels?

To: The Quest 2300 Team
From: Quest Central
Date: The year 2300
Subject: Mission Accomplished

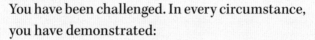

You have been challenged. In every circumstance, you have demonstrated:

- Integrity
- Perseverance
- Teamwork
- Professionalism

The Third Quest has prepared you to pursue your tomorrow. There is nothing you cannot achieve. You will continue to:

- Develop your inquiring mind
- Gain knowledge
- Weigh evidence
- Draw informed conclusions

Everyone was silent, thinking of the future. Mindy said, "No matter what, we stick together." Everyone nodded.

With that, the Quest 2300 team was transported into a crowd of cheering people. Twelve parents were waiting . . . hugs, laughter, and a big parade. •• Where is the team? •• What do you think the team members will do next?

Epilogue

Forty Years Later

Lambert is an ancient history scholar specializing in translating Indus Valley writing. Kate is a high school teacher. She was best teacher of the year in 2335.

The Quest 2300 team continues to meet once a year. Each team member works to fulfill a destiny set in motion by Quest Central and Dr. X. Bella will never be forgotten.

The Quest 2300 Team

Zack Jefferson
Supreme Court Justice of the United States
(Parents found not guilty in 2300)

Anna Gomez
4-Star General, Marine Corps

Ling Roberts
Medical research scientist, Nobel Prize winner in medicine

Shack Jones
Astronaut, flying mission to colonies on Mars

J.T. Tuppins
Senior Engineer, Quest Central
Finding water solutions, nominated for Nobel Prize in science (Meets frequently with Lambert to work on translations of Indus Valley writings)

Mindy Herzig, Director of Quest Central
Special Project: The safe return of the Quest 2200 team

• • •

Special Note: Tuppins and Mindy are married and have two children. •• Are you surprised about any of the outcomes for the Quest 2300 team?

The Quest 2200 Team

The Quest 2200 team continues to travel, following human migration patterns. When they reach the present, their quest will be completed successfully.

• • •

The Important When: Unknown
The Important Where: Unknown

Ronaldo, Cody, Jasmine, Bella, Lani, and Barack were startled by their sudden transport but happy to be reunited. Cody looked around, wondering where they were. Ronaldo said, "There's probably a memo somewhere. In fact, there's a folder under the *Beelzebufo.*"

Jasmine said, "Has he eaten lately?"

Bella said, "No problem. *Beelzebufo* has gotten pretty mellow."

Jasmine reached for the folder and said, "Okay, let's find out where we are."

Cody said, "Drum roll . . ." •• What can you predict for the 2200 team? How will you find out?